Stirring Up Additional
Success

with a

Southern Flavor

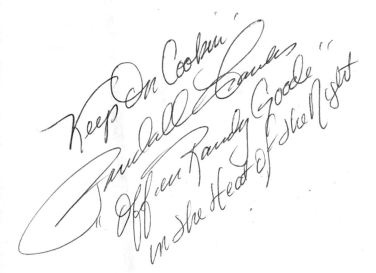

1

Stirring Up Additional Success

with a

Southern Flavor

A Friends of Literacy Cookbook

Randall Franks
and Shirley Smith

Published by the Catoosa Citizens for Literacy
36 Muscogee Trail
Ringgold, Ga. 30736   **ISBN 0-9668034-8-5**
Phone (706) 965-8275

Celebrity photographs used in this book were used by permis-
sion of the artists, actors, athletes or their representatives. All
photo copyrights remain with copyright holders.
Some historical photos appear courtesy of the George Hendrix
collection.
Hendrix copies historical images of interest concerning
Catoosa County. Copies of his collection are available at the
Catoosa County Library and the Old Stone Church.
Some historical photos appear courtesy the Catoosa County
Historical Society at the Old Stone Church Museum (706)
935-5232.
"Two Dozen Brown Eggs" (book cover artwork) © 2007
Cathy Cooksey, Ringgold, Ga.

GRAMMY ® is a registered trademark of the National Academy of
Recording Arts & Sciences, Inc.
OSCAR ® and **ACADEMY AWARD** ® are registered trademarks
or service marks of the Academy of Motion Picture Arts and
Sciences.
EMMY ® is a registered trademark and service mark of the
Academy of Television Arts and Sciences.
Coca-Cola ® is a registered trademark Coca-Cola Company.
Country Music Hall of Fame ® is a registered trademark Country
Music Hall of Fame and Museum.
Grand Ole Opry ® is a registered trademark the Gaylord
Entertainment Co.
Kool-Aid ®, **Cool Whip** ® and **Jell-o** ® are registered trademarks
of Kraft Foods Inc.
Bacardi ® is a registered trademark of Bacardi & Company
Limited.
Duncan Hines ® is a registered trademark of Pinnacle Foods
Group Inc.
Shoney's ® is a registered trademark of Shoney's North America
Corp.

Stirring Up Additional Success

with a

Southern Flavor

Recipe Coordinator
Darla Crawford

Cover Artist
Cathy Cooksey

This book is dedicated to the teachers
who enlighten by opening windows on the world
for all who strive to improve themselves through
learning to read.

Thank you for supporting **Stirring Up Additional Success with a Southern Flavor.**

As an actor and singer you quickly learn the importance of each word you say or sing. Many cannot even pick up a church hymnal to read the words of "Amazing Grace" or even scan the want ads for a job because they have never learned to read. I was honored when Shirley Smith asked me to help create a second cookbook as a fundraiser for the Catoosa Citizens for Literacy (CCL).

I see on a daily basis in my hometown how this organization is making a difference in the lives of the people of Appalachia. More than

Photo: Terry Pennington

Randall Franks

11,000 adults in our county do not have their high school dipomas and many cannot read or have reading difficulties.

Catoosa Citizens for Literacy is a 501-c3 Certified Literate Community Program. The mission of Catoosa Citizens for Literacy is to help families improve their lives by providing skills that will allow them to get a job, open other employment opportunities or simply be able to sit a child or grandchild upon their knee and read them a bedtime story.

Through the help of the local governments, grants, businesses and individuals, the CCL was able to construct The Learning Center, a facility to assist individuals in need of educational opportunities. The Learning Center provides GED classes, a tutoring program, a reading program, English Language Proficiency classes, and basic computer classes, all at no charge. Free childcare and transportation are provided as well. Through the help of fundraisers, such as this cookbook, Catoosa Citizens for Literacy funds the programs and services we offer, as well as funding the a program that pays $65 of the $95 GED testing fee for county residents.

I hoped that Shirley and I could once again gather the support of many of our old and new friends from TV, music and public service to help make this book something more than just another cookbook.

I am pleased that the response was outstanding and we added many film and television favorites. We would like to thank each and every one of those who participated.

Many have asked me why I share my time with the CCL. The reason is simple. I was blessed that I had two very intelligent parents Floyd and Pearl Franks who did not graduate from school because in their time they had to go to work to support themselves and their families at a young age. They both were self-educated and succeeded and excelled despite lack of high school diplomas. My father became a G.E.D. recipient. While my mother never did, her life and business successes far outweighed not having those credentials.

They knew the barriers that they had to overcome to succeed, so they spent their lives investing and encouraging youth to pursue higher education. Of course, my brothers and I were the focus of much of that energy but many youth benefited from their efforts.

Because of their encouragement, to my knowledge, I became the first of several in our families to graduate from college. So I know through shared experience what life can be without an education. Through watching the emotional and economic effects of not knowing how to read experienced by other family members, I saw how the lack of that skill could limit the possibilities of your life.

We especially want to give our appreciation to Darla Crawford. Her dedication to assist Shirley and me in collecting and compiling the nearly 200 recipes is really what made this project happen.

The historical references in this book were collected from oral histories, historical markers and previous press reports. I am sure that somewhere along the line some of this information came through the diligent work of Catoosa County's preservationists and historians at the Catoosa County Historical Society, Fort Oglethorpe Preservation Society and Catoosa County historian William H.H. "Bill" Clark. Thank you for your continued efforts to keep history alive.

Randall Franks *Past Chairman and Co-Chairman, Catoosa Citizens for Literacy Task Force Member 2001-2009*

Contributors

AT&T Wireless
BBC Foundation - Knox Farmer
The Braden Group/Bedford Place
Apartments
Catoosa County Government
City Of Fort Oglethorpe
Fuller Rehabilitation And Independent
Living Aids
Georgia Northwestern Technical College
Kiwanis Club of Fort Oglethorpe
Kiwanis Club of Ringgold
Northwest Georgia Bank
Randall Franks
Ringgold Telephone Company
Rotary Club of Ringgold
Roger & Kay Bowman
Roper Corporation
Wesley Smith
Weeks & Peters Insurance

Catoosa Citizens for Literacy Officers

2009-2010
Knox Farmer, Co-chairman;
Theresa McKamey, Co-chairman; Lynn Latimer,
Treasurer; Jackie Goolsby, Secretary
2008-2009
Randall Franks, Co-chairman;
Knox Farmer, Co-chairman
Lynn Latimer, Treasurer; Theresa McKamey, Secretary

Collaborative Partners:

Catoosa County Board Of Education

Catoosa County Chamber Of Commerce

Catoosa County Family Collaborative

Catoosa County Health Department

Catoosa County Library

The Catoosa County News

Catoosa County Pre-K Program

Catoosa County Sheriff's Department

Communities In Schools

Department Of Family And Children Services

Family Resource Agency Of North Georgia - Head
Start

Ferst Foundation for Childhood Literacy

Hutcheson Medical Center

Share America Foundation, Inc.

UCTV-3

Catoosa Citizens for Literacy Taskforce Members

Bacon

Everett

Ledbetter

Cirlot

Fowler

Eaker

Regina Bacon, Catoosa County Schools - Title 1
Donna Blevins, Head Start
Anna Marie Braden, Braden Group - Bedford Place Apts.
Bridgid Broderick, Catoosa County Library
Amy Carroll, Catoosa County Health Department
Marcy Cirlot, Ringgold Telephone Company
Darla Crawford, Catoosa County Learning Center
Paul Croft, Retired
Grace Davis, Catoosa County Schools
Mary Ann Dyer, Northwestern Technical College
Martha Eaker, Catoosa County Chamber of Commerce
Jayme Elliott, Communities In Schools
Brenda Evans, Hutcheson Medical Center
Nancy Everett, Tutor
Knox Farmer, Northwest Georgia Bank
Jim Fowler, Northwestern Technical College
Randall Franks, Share America Foundation, Inc.
Jackie Goolsby, Georgia Department of Labor
Beckie Hatcher, Tutor
Mike Helton, Catoosa County Manager
Melissa Holcombe, Catoosa County Schools
Lynn Latimer, Victory Signs
Phil Ledbetter, Family Collaborative
Theresa McKamey, Catoosa County Pre-K
Pat Page, Ringgold Rotary
Nancy Peters, Weeks & Peters Insurance
Donna Pierce, Northwestern Technical College
Denia Reese, Catoosa County Schools
Shirley Smith, Catoosa Citizens for Literacy
Jill Van Dyke, Catoosa County Health Department

The Learning Center Staff

Georgia Northwestern Technical College Staff:
Eveline Bryant - Paraprofessional
Mary Ann Dyer - GED Instructor
Dennis Dyer - Paraprofessional
Jim Fowler - Director
Donna Pierce - GED Instructor
Phillip Whiteside - English As Second Language

Childcare Providers:
Karen Austin
Lacey Goolsby
Stacy Newton
Charlotte Pierce
Rachel Wilson

Bus Driver:
Larry Renfro

Administrative Staff:
Shirley Smith, Executive Director
Darla Crawford, Educational Coordinator

The Learning Center offers assistance to those who want to learn to read. Free day and evening GED classes are available. The $65 of the $95 test fee is free to Catoosa County residents who take a minimum of 12 hours of GED instruction and remain in class until ready to take the test. ESL classes are offered. Georgia Northwestern Technical College offers a variety of classes, credit and non-credit, at the facility. Childcare and transportation are available at no charge. Contact the Learning Center for schedules (706) 965-6155.

Tutors And Volunteers

Reading:

Joanne Ritchie
Nancy Everett
Emenda Crowe
Kay Davenport
Grace Davis
Diane Griffith
Margaret Houck
Kerri Jenkins
Joan Jolley
Charlotte Pierce

Writing:

Barbara Tucker

Math:

Bill McDonald
Elaine Parkerson
Charles Smith

ESL:

Rachel Brown

Childcare:

Taylor Carter
Chelsey Guffey

Computer Class:

David Austin
B.J. Darnelle
Lacey Goolsby

Where Things Are Down South

Breaking the Literacy Barrier in Catoosa and

Catoosa County Learning Center expands

By Randall Franks

Accolades, awards, senatorial and gubernatorial visits all highlight the significance the program has gained amongst its colleagues in adult education.

The Learning Center before expansion

Whether its an adult trying to overcome a lifetime of not being able to read, a single mother looking to complete her general education development, someone desiring to learn to speak English, a family bread winner wishing to gain computer skills to improve their job opportunities, the center provides these and many other programs.

After eight years in its current facility the new addition is complete.

"Our primary limitation since we opened here was space," said Shirley Smith, executive director. "Trying to keep up with requests from students wanting to improve their opportunities in life through one of our programs far exceeded the facilities within our first few months."

The program filled every nook and cranny of the building with one of its many offerings attempting to give students a chance for a new lease on life, she said.

"The expansion allows us to provide an even more unique facility giving us the chance to better serve family literacy throughout our community," she said.

With the addition 4,100 square feet funded by a $500,000 state grant from Governor Sonny Perdue secured by state Sen. Jeff Mullis and Rep. Jay Neal, the program added education space in the form of class and conference rooms, a kitchen area and office space for the Catoosa Family Collaborative, which brings together all the various organizations in Northwest

ADDITION GRAND OPENING

The Catoosa County Learning Center welcomed dignitaries from across the region to the grand opening of the new addition to the facility in August 2009. Lt. Gov. Casey Cagle was the keynote speaker joined by State Sen. Jeff Mullis and State Rep. Jay Neal. (Photos by Randall Franks)

(Photo by Mark Andrews/ Catoosa County News)

Sen. Jeff Mullis

State Rep. Jay Neal

Phil Erli

Lt. Gov. Casey Cagle

Breaking the Literacy Barrier in Catoosa and

The Learning Center today

Georgia to better serve children and families.

Phil Ledbetter, Family Collaborative coordinator, is excited about partnering with the Learning Center in the new addition.

He said the space allows their organization to bring its programs all under one roof - its monthly meetings, nurturing parenting program and its teen council, which teaches leadership and team building skills to youth.

"It is going to be nice to be centrally located in the county," he said.

Due to the increase in construction costs since the process began, we have had to scale down the size of the expansion from 5,000 to 4,100 square feet, Smith said.

Construction costs were kept at a minimum by using a Georgia Department of Corrections construction crew for parts of the project, she said.

According to Darla Crawford, educational coordinator, literally thousands of students have made use of the facilities since it's opening. In 2007, 146 students successfully completed their GEDs.

The Catoosa Citizens for Literacy operate the Learning Center in cooperation with the county. The organization strives to bring down barriers from success at the facility by raising funds to make the programs more accessible.

"Eliminating the barriers to succeed in one's goals is the key to finding a better life," Smith said. "What we try to do is get rid of as many of those potential barriers as possible then its up to the student to make their own success story. This new building should bring a lot of those stories to Catoosa County."

PRETESTING YOUR TASTEBUDS
(APPETIZERS, BREADS & BEVERAGES)

ADDITION GRAND OPENING

CATOOSA COUNTY COURTHOUSE IN THE 1930'S

Catoosa's Mary Lynn Clark (not pictured) added to the collection of George Hendrix this mid-1930s photo of the historic Catoosa County Courthouse that served as a hospital during the Civil War. Clark went to work at the courthouse after graduating from business school in 1934. "I worked in all the different offices," she said. "I was one of the first in Ringgold that could type; they did not teach it in high school at that time. I worked for Jim Evitt, Clerk of the Court, but would work a day in each office." Clark remembers the courthouse being open and airy when you raised the windows. "People would often come up to you and visit through the windows," she said. "Court week was always exciting. Farmers from across the county would come in and often spend the whole week. People often invited them to stay in their homes."
Catoosa County leaders are (from left) Earl Carter of The Catoosa County Record; Bill Fuller, Justice of the Peace; Sheriff J.M. Moreland; Commissioner Ira McDaniel; (unidentified); Jim Evitt, Clerk of Court; Bill McClure, attorney; Ruth Williams, School Superintendent; Enoch West, Tax Commissioner; Charlie Vosburg, Ordinary; and Commissioners G.M. McDaniel, Jake Kellerhals, and Gene Combs.
(Photo from George Hendrix Collection/Catoosa County Historical Society)

PRETESTING YOUR TASTEBUDS

Ray Charles

From meager beginnings in Albany, Georgia, the late Ray Charles climbed the ladder of success to reach international stardom. Along the way, he won Hall of Fame memberships for Rhythm & Blues, Rock 'n' Roll, and Jazz. Early in his life, at the state school for the deaf and blind in St. Augustine, Florida, Charles learned to read Braille and type, and he developed and cultivated his interest in music. While he amassed countless hits in many genres and is a multiple GRAMMY® winner, on his musical journey throughout the years, Ray Charles could say that he always kept "Georgia On My Mind."

Artichoke Spread

1 can (14oz) artichoke hearts
½ cup sour cream
½ cup mayonnaise
1 cup parmesan cheese
pepper
garlic
salt

Preheat oven to 350. Chop artichoke hearts finely. I shred them in the food processor. Mix together with sour cream, mayonnaise and parmesan cheese. Add pepper and garlic salt to taste. Spread mixture into a shallow baking dish. Bake at 350° for 20-25 minutes or until golden on top. Spread on crackers or Ritz Crisps.

Vanessa Channell, Ringgold Primary School

PRETESTING YOUR TASTEBUDS

Celebration Cheeseball

8 oz cream cheese, softened
16 oz sharp cheddar cheese, shredded
¼ cup onion, finely diced
2 tbsp garlic, minced
3 tbsp Worcestershire sauce
1 tsp mustard
½ tbsp celery salt
1 tbsp garlic powder
1 tbsp onion powder
1/3 cup pecans, chopped

In a medium bowl, mix all ingredients except cheeses and pecans. Add cream cheese. Mix well. Gradually add shredded cheese, blending well and kneeding with hands if necessary. For softer mixture, add less shredded cheese. Shape mixture into a ball. Roll ball in pecans, coating on all sides. Serve cold.

Rachel Brown, Dalton Daily Citizen, ESL Volunteer

Cheese Ball for Veggies

3 (8oz) pkgs reduced fat cream cheese
1 envelope Hidden Valley Ranch Dip mix
1 ½ cup pecans, chopped

Mix cream cheese, dip mix and ½ cup pecans. Shape into a ball and roll in remaining pecans. Serve with assorted raw vegetables and crackers. Also works well as a stuffing for celery.

Donna Blevins, Head Start

PRETESTING YOUR TASTEBUDS

Morgan Freeman

Cheese Ball with Raspberry Preserves

½ lb American cheese
½ lb cheddar cheese
1 cup pecan chips
5 or 6 green onions, chopped
Mayonnaise
1 – 6 oz. jar raspberry preserves

In the early 1970s, Morgan Freeman electrified children with the "Easy Reader" from the series *The Electric Company*. The show provided children a fun way to learn while watching television. Since then, the three-time Academy Award® nominee has become one of America's most highly regarded actors.

In 1989, not only did Freeman land his first Academy Award® nomination for his role as the indomitable chauffeur Hoke Colburn in *Driving Miss Daisy*, but he also starred in *Lean On Me*, portraying Eastside High School principal Joe Clark. Through his unorthodox approach, Clark created a safe learning environment and encouraged students to succeed. Among some of Freeman's outstanding performances are roles in *Street Smart*, *The Shawshank Redemption*, *Glory*, *Outbreak* and *Seven*.

Grate American and cheddar cheese. Mix in pecan chips, chopped green onions and enough mayonnaise to hold together; pack into a mold or make into a ball. Refrigerate until ready to use. Unmold on tray and cover with raspberry preserves. Serve with crackers.

Jan Hendrix

24

Annette Newton's Chicken Cheese Ball

1 pkg (8oz) cream cheese
1 can (12oz) boneless chicken breast
1 can (4oz) boneless chicken breast
1 pkg ranch salad dressing mix (dry)
2 tbsp mayonnaise
Garlic powder to taste
Chopped pecans

Drain chicken breast. Mix softened cream cheese, mayo, garlic powder, and ranch dressing mix together. Add chicken and mix well. Roll in plastic wrap and chill. Roll in pecans before serving. This is also good to just add pecans to the mixture and use as a spread. Serve with assorted crackers.

Donna Blevins,
Head Start

Donna Blevins
CCL Task Force member
Position:
Family Partnership Manager, Family ResourceAgency of North Georgia
Reason for serving on the Task Force:
I facilitate trainings for family advocates for the Head Start Program. There are so many issues that our families encounter that can be solved or improved by edu cation. The Learning Center removes many of the barriers that can stand in the way of individuals who wish to finish their education. I was hon ored when asked to join the taskforce because we can work together to help provide a link to those most in need of the services that the Learning Center provides.
Organizations and Memberships:
Catoosa Citizens for Literacy, Cloverdale Baptist Church
Favorite movie:
Pretty Woman
Favorite book:
"The Rainmaker" John Grisham
Favorite TV show:
Dead Men Talking, Cold Case
Favorite quote:
"Never doubt that a small group of thoughtful commit ted citizens can change the world; indeed, it is the only thing that ever has." – Margaret Mead

PRETESTING YOUR TASTEBUDS

"We cannot learn without pain."
Aristotle

Chocolate Chip Cheeseball

1 pkg (8oz) cream cheese, softened
¼ tsp vanilla extract
½ cup butter, softened (no substitutes)
¾ cup confectioner's sugar
2 tbsp brown sugar
¾ cup miniature chocolate chips
¾ cup pecans, finely chopped
Graham Crackers

In a mixing bowl, beat the cream cheese, butter and vanilla until fluffy. Gradually add sugars; beat just until combined. Stir in chocolate chips. Cover and refrigerate for 2 hours. Place cream cheese mixture on a large piece of plastic wrap. Shape into a ball. Refrigerate for at least 1 hour. Just before serving, roll in pecans. Serve with graham crackers.

Donna Ledford

"Liberty without learning is always in peril and learning without liberty is always in vain."

President
John F. Kennedy

PRETESTING YOUR TASTEBUDS

Chubby Checker

Whether it's through radio, records, films or TV, Chubby Checker twisted himself into the hearts of fans beginning with his first song "The Twist" in 1959. Checker brought listeners hit after hit while adding to the long list of dances that teens and adults enjoyed such as the "The Fly," "The Pony" and "The Hucklebuck." Checker is the only artist to have five albums in the Top 12 all at once. He is the only artist to have a song, "The Twist," rise to the number 1 position twice. His first platinum release was "Let's Twist Again."
Today, he performs regularly and has an active snack food business making a variety of items such as Chocolate Checker Bars.
Visit www.chubbychecker.com

Christmas Cheese Ball

1 pkg (8oz) cream cheese, softened
2 cups cheddar cheese, shredded
2 green onions, chopped
1 jar pimentos, diced
2 tbsp butter, melted
2 tsp Worcestershire sauce

In a mixing bowl, beat cream cheese until fluffy. Beat in the cheddar cheese, onions, pimentos, butter and worcestershire sauce. Press into a small bowl; smooth top. Cover and refrigerate. Remove from the refrigerator 15 minutes before unmolding. Serve with assorted crackers.

Jan Hendrix

PRETESTING YOUR TASTEBUDS

Cheese Dip

1 lb lean ground beef
1 lb sausage (regular or hot)
1-8oz. cream cheese
1 can cream of mushroom soup
1 can cream of chicken soup
1 can Rotel tomatoes (w/ green chilies)
1 lb. Velveeta Cheese

Brown ground beef and sausage and drain well. Pour soups and Rotel tomatoes in a crock-pot, medium-high temperature. Cut the cream cheese and Velveeta and add, along with the beef and sausage to the crock-pot mixture. Cook in the crock-pot until all is melted and blended, stirring often. Serve with tortilla or corn chips.

Marcia Black
Ringgold Telephone Company

The Festival of Flags occurs in Ringgold in the weeks around Memorial Day and Veteran's Day where volunteers raise a flag and cross honoring over 800 deceased veterans who lived in the county. Visitors and residents such as Burl Franks (above) often search for the crosses honoring their loved ones.

PRETESTING YOUR TASTEBUDS

Columbian Salsa

8-10 Roma Italian tomatoes, peeled
1 small red onion
1 small sweet onion
1 small bell pepper
4-5 buttons garlic
½ bunch fresh parsley
1 hot pepper, optional
¼ cup olive oil
2 cups ketchup
1 tsp salt

Chop tomatoes, onions, garlic, hot pepper and bell pepper. Add remaining ingredients and stir. Cover and refrigerate overnight to allow flavors to develop. Serve with tortilla chips or as a relish with your favorite meat dishes.
Donna Pierce, GED Instructor

Corn Dip

1 can whole kernel corn, drained
1 pkg (8oz) cream cheese, softened
1 tomato, chopped (approx. 1 cup)
¾ cup Monterrey Jack/Colby cheese, shredded and divided
1 small jalapeno pepper, seeded and chopped finely

Preheat oven to 350°. Combine corn, cream cheese, tomato, ½ cup cheese and jalapeno. Spread into a greased 9" pie plate or casserole dish. Top with remaining ¼ cup cheese. Bake 25 minutes or until cheese is bubbly. Serve with party-style crackers.
Darla Crawford, Catoosa County Learning Center

Pee Wee King

With his Golden West Cowboys, the late Pee Wee King is credited with moving country music up-town and changing the way it is performed. From the ranks of his band came country superstars Eddy Arnold and Cowboy Copas. King left the *Grand Ole Opry* and established himself as a television star in TV's golden age. Along with band member Redd Stewart, King penned "Bonaparte's Retreat" and the crossover hit "The Tennessee Waltz." With Chilton Price the pair wrote the hit "Slow Poke."

King and his band appeared in several Gene Autry and Charles Starrett films such as *Ridin' the Outlaw Trail, Gold Mine in the Sky* and *The Rough Tough West*.

Pee Wee's Tennessee Waltzing Cheese Round

8 oz bleu cheese, softened to room temperature
3-8 oz packages cream cheese, softened to room temperature
1 jar of Old English cheese, softened to room temperature
2 tablespoons of Worcestershire sauce
1 cup ground pecans
1 small onion grated
1 cup dried or fresh parsley

Take the first six ingredients and mix well. Divide and shape into balls and roll on parsley. Cheese balls may be frozen. Makes two large or four small cheese balls.

Lydia King for Pee Wee King
Country Music Artist

PRETESTING YOUR TASTEBUDS

Edible Playdough
Great for kids to make!

1 cup peanut butter
1 cup oatmeal
1 cup powdered milk
1 cup honey
mixing bowl
waxed paper

Mix all ingredients together in the bowl using your hands. Pour mixture onto wax paper. Make shapes or roll into "snake" and pinch off sections and practice making letters, numbers, children's names, etc. When you're done playing with the edible play-dough, you can have a snack!

Theresa McKamey
Georgia Pre-K
Program
Catoosa Citizens for
Literacy Taskforce
Member

Theresa McKamey
CCL Task Force member
Position: Catoosa County Schools - Resource Coordinator for the Georgia Pre-K program

McKamey

Reason for serving on the Task Force: Promoting literacy is a focus in the Georgia Pre-K program. The literacy council and the staff at the Learning Center have always been supportive of the Catoosa County Schools Pre-K Program. The taskforce not only finds a way to provide services to our community and Pre-K families, but it also finds ways to break down the barriers that can keep people away by providing free classes, free child care, free tranportation and instructional and emotional support. All of our Pre-K children even receive a free "parent and child learning together t-shirt!" It is a pleasure to work with such helpful and enthusiastic people.

Organizations and Memberships: Member of First Baptist Church in Ringgold

Favorite movie: *O' Brother Where Art Thou*

Favorite book: *Love You Forever* - Sheila McGraw

Favorite TV show: *Star Trek*

Favorite quote: "Remember that happiness is a way of travel, not a destination." Roy M. Goodman

31

PRETESTING YOUR TASTEBUDS

Easy Appetizer

**8oz block cream cheese
Strawberry jam**

Open cream cheese and
place on pretty plate. Pour
strawberry jam on top.
Serve with crackers and
spreading knives.
Joy Thornton

Hot Pizza Dip

**1 pkg (8oz) cream cheese,
softened
1 tsp dried Italian seasoning
1 cup mozzarella cheese,
shredded
¾ cup parmesan cheese
1 can (8oz) pizza sauce
2 tbsp green pepper,
chopped
2 tbsp green onions, sliced**

Scott Bakula

While he is now appearing in
various films such as *The
Informant* or guesting on TV
shows such as *The New
Adventures of Old Christine*,
from 2001-05 Scott Bakula was
going where no man has gone
before in Paramount's Star Trek
series *Enterprise*, playing the role
of Captain Jonathan Archer. He
won a Golden Globe in 1992 for
"Best Performance by an Actor
in a TV-Series-Drama for his role
as Dr. Sam Beckett in *Quantum
Leap.*

Preheat oven to 350° F. Combine cream cheese and Italian seasonings , spread onto a 8" mini-baker. In a small bowl, combine mozzarella and parmesan. Sprinkle 1/2 on top of the
cream cheese. Spread pizza sauce over the cheese mixture.
Sprinkle with remaining cheese. Top with bell pepper and
green onions. Bake for 15-18 minutes. Serve with French
bread or fresh vegetable dippers.
Vanessa Channell, Ringgold Primary School

Northwest Georgia Bank Amphitheatre Sunset Concert Series

(Photo by Terry Pennington)

in 2007 marked a million dollar gift commemorating the bank's centennial. The free community appreciation, three-night concert series on July 26, 27, 28, sponsored by Northwest Georgia Bank, US101 and 98.1 - The Legend featured performances by John Anderson (above), Mt. Peria Baptist Choir, Heirline, Poet Voices, Joanna Cotten, Sarah Johns, Scott Smith and Friends, Roger Alan Wade and country duo Fanny Grace. "It's been a long journey full of a lot of hard work, a lot of brainstorming, and a lot of really dedicated individuals," said Wes Smith, Northwest Georgia Bank Chairman and CEO. "We are wholly grateful for the help and support we've had from many generous people over the years.... it is our earnest and adamant hope that local governments will in good faith and wise judgment continue to support with fervor these fine institutions dedicated to local arts, education and public service."

Wes Smith (right) turns the Amphitheatre keys over to, from left, Former Catoosa Commissioner Jim Emberson, and Catoosa Commissioners Dewayne Hill and Ken Marks.
(Photo by Stan Guess)

PRETESTING YOUR TASTEBUDS

Mac Stringer speaks to a class filled with adult students at the Catoosa County Learning Center.

Literacy picnic encourages success
By Randall Franks

Catoosa County Learning Center honored its students with an indoor literacy picnic Sept. 18, 2008 as part of the Literacy Month festivities at the center.

Donna Pierce, literacy instructor, told students it is a reward to honor their efforts in striving to achieve their educational goals. Several students also received certificates.

Former G.E.D. recipient Mac Stringer returned to the environment where he studied to inspire current students with a motivational talk. He represented the region in a statewide adult education competition a few years ago.

Stringer was a high school dropout at 15; in his 40s, he decided to pursue his general education development diploma to lay the foundation for a job in management, sales or working with computers.

He told students that they must make the decision to move forward with their lives. He said when he dropped out all his friends left him behind, although he did not see it at the time. They went on to make more successful lives than he could himself without the education, he said.

He told the students that he wanted to see them one day come back to the center and encourage other students to take the steps necessary to change their lives for the better. He said he owed the opportunities for learning to the staff of the Learning Center.

"They were always willing to help with problems we came against in the class, and they never made me feel less of a person," he said. "They let me know I can and I will, through hard work, get my GED."

Now he shares his enthusiasm for learning with others.

"Plains Special" Cheese Ring

1 lb grated sharp cheese
1 cup finely chopped nuts
1 cup mayonnaise
1 small onion, finely grated

Combine all ingredients, except preserves. Season to taste with pepper. Mix well and place in a 5 or 6 cup lightly greased ring mold. Refrigerate until firm for several hours or overnight. To serve, unmold, and if desired, fill center with strawberry preserves, or serve plain with crackers.

Rosalynn Carter
Former First Lady
of the United States

Rosalynn Carter

Former First Lady Rosalynn Smith Carter dedicates much of her time to improving the lives of people who are mentally or emotionally handicapped. Both in her home state of Georgia and on a national level, her work has resulted in the passage of laws such as the Mental Health Systems Act. Among her books are her autobiography, *First Lady from Plains*, *Everything to Gain: Making the Most of the Rest of Your Live*, which she co-authored, and *Helping Yourself Help Others*, which draws on her personal experiences as First Lady and as the Director of the Rosalynn Carter Institute for Human Development. In 1984, Mrs. Carter became a member of the board of advisors of Habitat for Humanity, Inc.

35

PRETESTING YOUR TASTEBUDS

Shirley Smith works to make a

difference in Catoosa County

By Randall Franks

Helping to improve the community in which she lives is not only a passion of Shirley Smith - it is her daily mission.

Smith became a member of Catoosa Citizens for Literacy in 1992.

In 1995, she became executive director after a period when the organization was about to be disbanded.

"Let me tell you how bad it was, " she said. " There was a $15 fee for something, and we bounced the check," she said.

When Smith took the job, there was a need for space for the adult literacy classes provided by Northwestern Technical College; otherwise, the county stood the chance of losing these classes.

"My gift, for lack of another word, is that I can get the word out there," she said. "I tell people that we have a 36.2 percent illiteracy rate here, which means there are 11,000 people in Catoosa County who do not have their high school diplomas."

In a matter of two years, the CCL, with Smith's leadership, raised $500,000 to build a new 5,500-square-foot Learning Center on Benton Place campus on Battlefield Parkway.

"When people know they will create results, they do give.

PRETESTING YOUR TASTEBUDS

Red Onion and Black Pepper Spread

1 pkg (8oz) cream cheese, softened
¼ cup finely chopped red onions
1 clove garlic, pan toasted, peeled and chopped
¼ tsp black pepper, coarsely ground
2 tbsp fresh parsley, chopped
Roasted Vegetable Ritz crackers

Mix cream cheese, onions, garlic and pepper until well blended. Shape into 6-inch log; wrap tightly in plastic wrap. Refrigerate 30 minutes or until firm. Roll in parsley until evenly coated on all sides. Serve as a spread with the crackers.

Shirley Smith, Executive Director Catoosa Citizens for Literacy

I think the program speaks for itself," she said. "Our mission is to provide a better-educated workforce for Catoosa County by helping citizens help themselves through education."
In the last year the center has helped many achieve their goal of attaining a GED.
Smith applied for and received a grant to purchase workstations for GED classes, equipment for reading, GED and computer classes, and computers for the computer lab, which offers free computer skills to Catoosa County citizens. An instructor was hired to provide free childcare for the children of GED students. In addition, an educational coordinator was employed to coordinate childcare, GED, English as a Second Language, and continuing education classes with Northwestern Technical College.
"Because of GED classes, childcare for GED students, ESL classes, reading classes that are taught by volunteers for those who have no reading skills or have difficulty reading, parenting classes and basic computer classes also taught by volunteers, the Learning Center stays very busy," she said.
"The result has been so overwhelming that the center is

PRETESTING YOUR TASTEBUDS

expanding again," she said. "My goal is to take away every barrier to getting a diploma."

The new building addition will be complete in the summer of 2009. Smith also found a way to pay $65 GED towards the $95 testing fee for all Catoosa County citizens and CCL purchased a $52,000 bus to transport students to the center. She also works with Northwestern Technical College and local businesses to provide workplace programs where employees can receive their GEDs while at work. She said her dream is for a young mother or father to be able to walk in the center, get child care while they get their GED, take some computer classes, enroll in Northwestern Technical College for continuing education, and eventually walk out of the center with a diploma, a degree, and good job, and a happy and prosperous family.

"I have always loved education," Smith said. "I always felt my family was blessed to be able to get one - but I felt bad, too, that some others weren't able to give themselves an education. When you are blessed, you should give back. And there is no place where you see such results from your giving. If you go to a graduation ceremony for GED recipients, it is just so touching."

Party or Shower Sandwiches

½ cup cream cheese, softened
½ cup whole berry cranberries
28 slices Pepperidge Farms cinnamon-raisin bread, crust cut off
28 thinly sliced ham (about 1 ¼ lbs)

Mix together cream cheese & cranberries. Place mixture and one slice of ham between two slices of bread.

Vanessa Channell

PRETESTING YOUR TASTEBUDS

Salmon Cheeseball

2 pkgs (8oz) cream cheese
1 large can pink salmon, drained and flaked
1 tbsp horseradish
3 or 4 splashes of Liquid Smoke (to taste)
½ chopped onion or 2 tbsp dried minced onion
1 tsp lemon juice
Finely chopped nuts (pecans)

Soften cream cheese and mix all ingredients together. Shape into ball, wrap in Saran wrap and refrigerate until firm. Roll in chopped nuts and serve with Ritz, Town House or saltine crackers.

Linda Burnett

Billy Crystal

Comedian, actor, director, producer, writer are all words attributed to the ever-talented Billy Crystal. He will host the Oscars in 2010 for a ninth time. Through his endless string of movie hits and television appearances, he has raised the level of comedy in America. Beginning as a mainstay on television in the 1970s and 80s in shows such as *Soap* and *Saturday Night Live*, one of his early film hits was *When Harry Met Sally*. Among the many film favorites are the two films highlighting "Mitch Robbins" and his friends as they go west in "City Slickers" and *City Slickers II: The Legend of Curly's Gold* and the mob-themed comedies *Analyze This* and *Analyze That*. He is starring in the new film *Tooth Fairy*.

39

Small Shrimp Quiches

½ cup butter
4 ozs cream cheese
2 tbsp cream
1 ¼ cups flour
½ tsp salt

Cream butter and cheese. Beat in the cream and add flour and salt, making a dough. Preheat oven to 425°. Roll out pastry and cut rounds to fit a muffin tin. Fit rounds into tin.

Cristy Lane

Inspirational singer Cristy Lane climbed the country charts in the 70s with songs such as "Shake Me I Rattle" and "I Just Can't Stay Married to You." She hit the top of the charts in 1979 when she showed millions how to live through the inspirational lyrics of the now multi-platinum "One Day At A Time." Lane's biography by the same name also became a best seller.
Visit www.cristylane.com.

1-2 cups cooked shrimp
1 ½ cups cream
3 eggs
1 cup Swiss cheesesalt and pepper
½ tsp dill weed
1 small onion, chopped
¼ tsp hot pepper

Chop shrimp and combine with cream, eggs, onions, cheese, salt and pepper and dill weed. Spoon shrimp mixture into muffin tin over pastry and bake 5 to 8 minutes. Turn heat down to 350° and bake another 15 minutes or so until golden brown.

Cristy Lane Country and Gospel Music Artist

PRETESTING YOUR TASTEBUDS

Spinach and Artichoke Dip

2 pkgs (8oz) cream cheese, softened
¾ cup half & half
1 tbsp onion, finely chopped
1 clove garlic, minced
½ cup parmesan cheese, grated
1 bag (10oz) frozen cut spinach, thawed and well drained
1 can (13 oz) quartered artichoke hearts, rinsed, drained and chopped
2/3 cup Monterey Jack cheese, shredded

Combine cream cheese and half & half in a bowl until well blended. Add the remaining ingredients, minus the grated cheese, and stir well. Pour the mixture into a crock-pot. Cover and cook on high for 1 ½ - 2 hours until warm. Sprinkle with parmesan cheese.
Cindie Robinson, Uniktings, Ringgold

Spinach Dip

1 bag frozen spinach, thawed
1 envelope onion soup mix
1 cup sour cream
1 cup mayonnaise
1 small block cream cheese, softened
1 cup cheese, shredded

Squeeze all liquid out of spinach, set aside. Mix sour cream, mayonnaise and cream cheese until well blended. Add soup mix, stir. Add spinach and shredded cheese. Mix well and chill. Place dip in a bread bowl before serving. Serve with bread cubes, crackers or raw veggies.
Gail Helton

Lady Bird Johnson

As an environmentalist, the late First Lady Claudia "Lady Bird" Johnson (1912-2007) worked to make her home state of Texas and her country a more beautiful place. While in Washington, she enlisted friends to help plant thousands of daffodils and tulips that continue to brighten our nation's Capital.

The Highway Beautification Act of 1965 was enacted as a result of her national campaign for beautification.

She authored A *White House Diary* and co-authored *Wildflowers Across America* with Carlton Lees.

(Photo courtesy LBJ Library by Frank Wolfe)

Spinach Parmesan

3 lbs spinach
6 tbsp Parmesan Cheese
6 tbsp minced onion
6 tbsp heavy cream
5 tbsp melted butter
½ cup cracker crumbs

Cook the cleaned spinach until tender. Drain thoroughly. Chop coarsely and add the cheese, onion, cream and 4 tbsp of the butter. Arrange in a shallow baking dish and sprinkle with the crumbs mixed with the remaining butter. Bake for 10 to 15 minutes.

Brandied Fruit

Dried Apricots
Golden Raisins
Pineapple Chunks
Canned Peaches
Whole Cranberries

Drain well pineapple chunks, peaches and cranberries. Layer fruit ending with cranberries. Dust with brown sugar, dab with sweet butter. Pour dry sherry over all. Bake in 350° oven for 20 minutes.

No measurements were given with this recipe. It's up to the cook!

Lady Bird Johnson
Former First Lady
of the United States

PRETESTING YOUR TASTEBUDS

Texas Caviar

2 cans black-eyed
peas
1 can shoe peg corn
1 can reg. rotel
tomatoes with
chilies
1 can chopped
green chilies
1 can petite diced
tomatoes
2 tbsp red onion,
finely minced
6 green onions,
chopped
2 garlic cloves,
chopped
1 poblano pepper,
chopped finely (you
can substitute bell
pepper)
Italian dressing (I
use Good
Seasonings made
with olive oil and
red wine vinegar)

Van Dyke

Jill Van Dyke

*CCL Task Force
Member*
Position: Program
Associate for the
Catoosa County
Health Department
**Reason for serving on
the Task Force:**
I am proud to be a
task force
member of such a great commu
nity supported program.
The Literacy Center provides an
educational resource for the citi
zens of our community that are
seeking to enhance their life
choices and opportunities. I
believe that the programs offered
at the Center not only enhance
the individuals on a personal
level but also provide an avenue
for them to become a more
productive citizen.
Organizations and memberships:
Local Emergency Planning
Committee,
Ringgold Parks Committee,
Chamber of Commerce,
Georgia Public HealthAssociation,
Catoosa Citizens For Literacy
Favorite movie: Dirty Dancing
Favorite book: too many to pick from
Favorite TV show: Anything on the
Food Network Channel

Chop all vegetables
finely and drain. Do
not use a food processor (makes too mushy). Add enough
dressing to make moist. Salt and pepper to taste. Serve with
large Frito scoops.
Jill Van Dyke – Literacy Taskforce Member

Carter Fuller sees encouraging adult education opportunities as a must for changing lives.

By Randall Franks

Carter Fuller encourages graduates at the 2008 Catoosa County G.E.D. graduation.

It was trying to correct a mistake that started Ringgold's Carter Fuller on the road he walks today.

He said that mistake was he dropped out of high school at 18. "I made a lot of errors as a young man and made a very unwise decision to drop out," he said. "It was devastating to my family and loved ones."

However, twenty years ago he probably could not envision being president and chief operating officer of Fuller Rehabilitation, Inc. or living with his wife Tera and their four children Haley, Jacob, Jordan and Caroline near Ringgold. Fuller Rehabilitation is a family company with hundreds of employees in locations across the country providing mobility power chairs, scooters and lift chairs to customers.

But before he could help lead this company, he had some other steps to take.

"What happened (after I dropped out) is I went to Walker Tech under great encouragement from my parents (Mike and Leila) to take my GED exam," he said. "At the time I did not realize

PRETESTING YOUR TASTEBUDS

how important that would be. That was a pathway into much greater and bigger things that happened later on in my life." His choice allowed him to join the U.S. Army which he served for four year including a period in Germany that allowed him to be

Chelsea Isbill receives the 2008 Carter Fuller Scholarship from Carter Fuller (right) and Randall Franks, CCL chairman.

present as the Berlin Wall came down marking the change of the world.

Deciding not to stay in the military, he returned home and began work. He pursued higher education with the aide of the GI Bill. He would not have reached this point without taking the GED, he said.

"Once I was married I was able then to go back to school as an adult learner at Dalton State College for a couple of years and then go to Covenant College and keep pursuing my education," he said.

He said it was during the same period the family business began and once his GI Bill ran out, his work for the business financed his way through the masters' program at the University of Georgia.

"The GED and adult education is a great opportunity for people to better themselves," he said. "It opens windows of opportunities for the people around them. It shows what hard work and education can do."

"I think it's an important thing," he said. "There are mistakes that are going to be made upon life's path. Every one of us, if we are all honest, goes the wrong direction. I see adult education

45

and things like the GED as a way for someone to have an opportunity to correct some wrongs."

Fuller believes it is only right people have the opportunity to make improvements to their life. He said he could not have fulfilled his role in the family business without having the chance to correct his mistake of dropping out of school. "We have 16 stores and we will have 18 before the end of year despite the economic downturn," he said. "We keep growing and doing pretty well. I am a blessed man. It all started with a decision to go to Walker Tech and get a GED." Fuller Rehabilitation supports the Catoosa County Learning Center with regular contributions and endows the Carter Fuller GED Scholarship Fund at the Learning Center providing a special scholarship for G.E.D. graduates.

Veggie Dip

1 (16 oz) sour cream
1 large block cream cheese, softened
1 cup cheddar cheese, shredded
1 pkg bacon bits
1 pkg dry Ranch dressing mix

Combine sour cream and cream cheese until smooth, add ranch mix. Stir well. Add bacon bits and shredded cheese. Mix well. Chill before serving. Use as a dip for veggies.

Gail Helton

PRETESTING YOUR TASTEBUDS

Wonderful Cheese Ball

2 pkgs (8oz) cream cheese
3 ½ cups sharp cheddar cheese, shredded
1 pkg ranch dressing mix
2 cups pecans, chopped
4 pecan halves

Mix together cream cheese, cheddar cheese, and dressing mix.
Form into one large ball or two smaller balls. Roll in chopped
pecans to cover. Decorate the top with pecan halves.
Refrigerate for at least a couple hours or overnight before
serving.

Jan Hendrix

Led by the city of Ringgold, the historic Ringgold Depot, one
of the few remaining antebellum railroad depots in the
Georgia, underwent a $650,000 preservation effort in 2002.
The building took tremendous damage during the Battle of
Ringgold Gap and was rebuilt. It was from the Ringgold Depot
that General Sherman led his troops through Ringgold Gap to
begin his campaign against Atlanta and the heart of the
South.
(Photo by Randall Franks)

PRETESTING YOUR TASTEBUDS

Barbecue Sauce

2 ½ cups catsup
½ cup vinegar
½ cup sugar
1 cup broth (beef or pork)
6-8 cloves of garlic
1 tbsp onion
2 ½ tsp Worcestershire sauce
¾ tsp red pepper
¾ tsp hot sauce
Bring to a boil and simmer a few minutes

Devona Hall was the Catoosa Learning Center 2006 Student of the Year. Hall is presented the award by co-chairpersons Ann Nix and Randall Franks.

Beckie Hatcher, CCL Task Force Member

Honolulu Soy Sauce

½ cup soy sauce
½ cup pineapple juice
¼ cup cooking oil (optional)
1 tsp dry mustard
1tbsp brown sugar
2 tsp ground ginger
1 tsp garlic salt
¼ tsp pepper
Combine all ingredients in saucepan. Simmer five minutes; cool. Marinate your favorite meat for one hour. Grill or broil for 20 minutes, basting with remaining sauce.

Alice Evitt Bandy
Ringgold Telephone Company

PRETESTING YOUR TASTEBUDS
BEVERAGES

Banana Slush Punch

6 cups hot water
4 cups sugar
1 large can pineapple juice
2 cans (12 oz) frozen orange juice, thawed
1 can (12 oz) frozen lemonade, thawed
6 ripe bananas, blended in a blender
3 (2 liters) ginger ale or Sprite

Dissolve sugar in water. Add pineapple juice, orange juice, lemonade & bananas. Freeze in three large containers. Take out of freezer 2 hours before serving. For each container of punch mixture, add 1 cold bottle of ginger ale (or Sprite).
Serve while slushy.
For smaller batch, ½ the recipe

Vanessa Channell

Country Music Hall of Fame members George Jones and Virginia Wynette Byrd (Tammy Wynette) tied the knot at the Catoosa County Courthouse February 25, 1969.

CCL Task Force member Phil Ledbetter adds a lot of fun to special events such as the Catoosa Ferst Foundation for Childhood Literacy Adult Spelling Bee.

PRETESTING YOUR TASTEBUDS

Carlos Santana "Smooth"-i.e.

1 banana, sliced
5-6 strawberries, sliced
8 oz vanilla yogurt
12 oz orange juice
1 tbsp almonds, finely sliced

Combine ingredients in a blender and mix for 30 seconds.
Pour and serve.
Note: for a "Berry Smooth" smoothie, add 1 handful of blue-
berries to the above recipe.
Tommy Housworth, Actor/writer

Tommy Housworth

Tommy Housworth is a commercial actor who has appeared
in numerous projects for the Georgia Lottery, Beautyrest,
Comcast and the Cartoon Network and in over 200 corporate
videos. He has authored two books *Smirking into the Abyss*
and *Welcome to Storyville*.

"Live as if you were to die tomorrow.
Learn as if you were to live forever."

Gandhi (1869-1948)

R
I
N
G
G
O
L
D

G
E
O
R
G
I
A

Above: This early 1900s photo of Ringgold was donated to the city by the family of Franklin P. Tucker who was stationed at the Army Post in Fort Oglethorpe. Below: The historic district of Ringgold has been the focal point of downtown since the 1800s. The city was named for Mexican War hero Major Samuel Ringgold who died of wounds following the Battle of Palo Alto in 1846.

(Photo by Randall Franks)

PRETESTING YOUR TASTEBUDS

Cherry Limeade Punch

1 Cherry-Limeade Sherbet (Mayfield)
1-1 ½   2 liters sprite, chilled
1 small jar maraschino cherries

Charlotte Pierce
CCL Task Force Member
Position: Childcare Provider
Favorite movie: The Princess Bride
Favorite book: "The Illiad"
Favorite TV show: House

Pierce

Pour sprite over sherbet and add jar of cherries for a little kick.

Chocolate-Vanilla Coffee Punch

1 half gallon chocolate ice cream (Mayfield works best because it is so creamy)
1 half gallon vanilla ice cream
6 cups very strong day old coffee, chilled
Whipped cream
Chocolate syrup (for drizzling)

Thaw ice cream for thirty minutes on the counter and then pour chilled coffee over both half gallons in punch bowl, top with whipped cream and drizzle with chocolate syrup.

Vanessa Channell, Ringgold Primary School

PRETESTING YOUR TASTEBUDS

Hawaiian Lemonade

1 can (6oz) frozen lemonade concentrate
1 can (12 oz) apricot nectar, chilled
1 can (12 oz) pineapple juice, chilled
1 can (12 oz) ginger ale, chilled
5 fresh pineapple wedges
5 lime slices
5 maraschino cherries

In a large pitcher combine lemonade concentrate and one can of water. Add apricot nectar and pineapple juice. Slowly pour ginger ale down the side of the pitcher. Stir gently with an up and down motion to mix. Serve over ice with pineapple, lime, and cherries skewered on a wooden pick. Brisk and refreshing!!

Delores Turner

Mocha Punch

5 heaping tsp instant decaf Coffee
3 cups boiling water
6 tbsp chocolate syrup
1 quart milk
½ gallon vanilla ice cream, softened

Mix coffee & water. Add choc syrup. Cool overnight in fridge. When ready to serve, pour into punch bowl then add milk & ice cream.

Vanessa Channell, Ringgold Primary School

Punch

**2 pkgs flavored kool aid
2 cups sugar
2 qts water
1 bottle ginger ale
1 can pineapple juice**

Mix kool aid, sugar and water, then freeze. Use a bundt pan if you have one. Set frozen mixture out to semi thaw. Place in large punch bowl. Pour ginger ale and pineapple juice over the semi thawed mixture to form a slushy tangy, very good treat.

Wilma Hopper

Charo

The multi-award winning flamenco guitarist, singer, actor, comedienne is a household name around the world. She is currently starring in "Charo in Concert: A Musical Sensation" at the Riviera Hotel & Casino in Las Vegas. Her latest musical hit España Caní won her a 2009 World Dance Music Award Nomination. With her expression "Cuchi-Cuchi," she was a mainstay on 1970s and 80s television who continues to wow audiences on shows such as *The Surreal Life* on VH1. She is a Screen Actors Guild Award and Billboard International Latin Music Award winner. Visit www.charo.com.

PRETESTING YOUR TASTEBUDS
BREADS

Banana Nut Bread

3 ripe bananas, mashed
2 cups flour
2 eggs slightly beaten
½ cup butter or oleo
1 cup white sugar
1 tsp soda
1 tsp vanilla
1 cup nuts, chopped
¼ tsp salt

(Photo: Bridge Mihalik)

Stella Parton

In a large mixing bowl, cream butter/oleo and sugar. Add eggs and vanilla. Add flour, salt and soda. Add bananas and nuts. Pour into greased and floured pans. Bake 350° 35 to 40 minutes.

Stella Parton

Country Music

Artist/Actress

Stella Parton gives *Testimony* with her latest CD, her single "Family Ties" rose in the top 20 UK Music Charts. Since her first hit single, "I Want to Hold You in My Dreams Tonight," through 22 albums and 24 chart singles, plus numerous awards and nominations, Stella has touched millions. With her unique ability to relate with people in all walks of life, she devotes herself to special causes such as domestic violence. She helps women build self-esteem by sharing her knowledge of hair and make up at the New Opportunity School for Women in Berea, Kentucky. As a stage, film and television actress, Stella has starred in numerous projects. Her works include *Seven Brides for Seven Brothers*, *Gentlemen Prefer Blondes*, *Cloud Dancer* and *The Color of Love* with Lou Gossett, Jr., and Gina Rowlands. She is also a talented chef and cookbook author.
Visit www.stellaparton.com.

PRETESTING YOUR TASTEBUDS

Broccoli Cornbread

2 boxes Jiffy corn muffin mix
1 cup margarine
6 large eggs
½ tsp salt
12 oz cottage cheese
2 cups broccoli, cooked and chopped
1 large chopped onion

Mix all ingredients together and pour into greased 13x9 inch pan. Bake at 350° for 40 minutes or until top is lightly browned.

Joy Thornton

Easy Banana Nut Bread

3 eggs
½ cup margarine, melted
3 small bananas, mashed
½ cup water
1 tbsp vanilla
1 pkg (18 ½ oz) yellow cake mix
1 cup chopped pecans

"Reading is very important because you learn things that you wouldn't learn otherwise. It brings back memories that has long been forgotten. The role that a grand mother or great-grandmother plays is very important in a family history as well as in the history of the church. This is the reason why the Adult Learning Center is so important. P. S. I am 96 years old"

Roberta Boyd

Combine eggs, margarine, bananas, water and vanilla in large mixing bowl; mix thoroughly. Stir in cake mix; beat well. Stir in nuts. Pour into greased and floured 10-inch tube pan. Bake in 350° oven for 50 minutes, or until golden.

Roberta Boyd

PRETESTING YOUR TASTEBUDS

Banana Bread

1 cup sugar
2 cups plain four, unsifted
½ cup margarine
3 tbsp sour cream
2 eggs, separated
1 tsp soda
½ tsp salt
4 ripe bananas
1 tsp vanilla flavoring

Cream margarine, add egg yolks and sugar. Add flour, salt, soda, sour cream, and bananas. Beat egg whites, fold into mixture. Add vanilla flavoring. Pour into greased loaf pan. Cook at 350° for one hour or until done.

Ann Nix, CCL Task Force Past Chair

Encouraging the class of 2018 with a desire to graduate

Shirley Smith, Catoosa County Learning Center executive director, asks Boynton Elementary third graders what they wish to be when they grow up. The Catoosa Citizens for Literacy are working to encourage Catoosa youth to commit to graduating by giving them their first graduation gift. The organization is trying to start at the ground level and get kids to make the commitment to finish school. The organization is presenting each member of the class of 2018, third graders, with their own dictionary which also provides study references for many of the subjects the children will be learning over the next few years such as geography, civics, mathematics and chemistry. One CCL Task Force representative wearing a cap and gown presented the students at each school with a dictionary, a Learning Center pen and a bookmark. Each student is able to write their name in their own dictionary to keep and use for years to come. (Photo by Randall Franks)

57

Hawaii Banana Nut Bread

3 cups plain flour
1 tsp soda
1 tsp salt
1 tsp cinnamon
1 cup nuts, (I use English Walnuts)
3 eggs, beaten
1 ½ cup oil
1 can (8oz) crushed pineapple
2 cups sugar
2 tsp vanilla
2 cups mashed bananas

Stonewall Jackson

Preheat oven to 350°. Mix together flour, soda, salt, cinnamon, and nuts. Set aside. In separate bowl, beat together eggs, oil, pineapple, sugar, vanilla, and bananas. Stir in dry ingredients until moist. Makes one bundt pan or three coffee can size. Bake 50 to 60 minutes or line five mini loaf pans (2"x5"x3") with wax paper and bake 45 minutes in 350° oven.

Stonewall Jackson
Country Music Artist

Grand Ole Opry star Stonewall Jackson, who grew up in South Georgia, has performed as part of the famed show since 1956. With around 40 hits to his credit including his career song "Waterloo" he has developed a legion of fans who love his straight-forward country sound. Other famous songs include "Don't Be Angry," "B.J. the D.J.," and "I Washed My Hands in Muddy Water." Jackson made a statement in 2006 when he sued the ownership of the Opry claiming age discrimination. The suit was settled in 2008 and Jackson returned to the Opry stage. He received the Ernest Tubb Memorial Award in 1997.

PRETESTING YOUR TASTEBUDS

English Scones

2 ½ cups flour
1 cup sugar (I use Splenda for baking)
1 cup shortening
1 cup golden raisins
1 tsp baking powder
1 ¾ cup milk (approx.)

Cut shortening flour until mixture resembles fine crumbs. Add sugar, baking powder, and raisins, and combine well. Add enough milk to make a light dough. Roll out about one-half inch thick on floured surface, and cut with biscuit cutter. Place on ungreased baking sheet, and bake for 10 to 15 minutes or until nicely browned.

Marcia Kling
Television journalist

Marcia Kling

A Chattanooga television news anchor, who became "Miss Marcia" on *Romper Room* in 1962, developed *Fun Time* airing 1963-1978 and then *Nifty Nine*. She hosted and produced *Weekend* in 1981. She is currently WTVC NewsChannel 9's LifeWatch reporter and co-anchor of *THIS n THAT*. She is the recipient of the Pilot Club 2001 Woman's Community Service Award, 1997 Woman of Distinction, and 2006 Mary Lou Wojick Memorial Angel of Giving Award presented by Partnership for Families, Children and Adults Auxiliary.

PRETESTING YOUR TASTEBUDS

Hawaiian Banana Nut Bread

3 cups all-purpose flour
2 cups sugar
1 tsp salt
1 tsp soda
1 tsp ground cinnamon
1 cup walnuts or pecans, chopped
3 eggs, beaten
1 ½ cup vegetable oil
2 cups ripe bananas, mashed
1 can (8oz) crushed pineapple, drained –reserve liquid
2 tsp vanilla extract

Combine dry ingredients, stir in nuts and set aside. Combine remaining ingredients and add in dry ingredients stirring until batter is moistened. Spoon batter into two greased and floured loaf pans. Drizzle reserved juice over bread as it cools. Cool 10 minutes before removing from the pans. Freezes well.

Donna Blevins, Head Start

"No matter how busy you may think you are, you must find time for reading, or surrender yourself to self-chosen ignorance."

- Confucius

PRETESTING YOUR TASTEBUDS

Mexican Cornbread

1 ½ cup corn meal
1 ½ tbsp sugar
½ tsp salt
¾ cup cheddar cheese, grated
3 oz oil
5 oz milk
1 egg
½ can cream style corn
Jalapenos to taste

Place a dab of oil/shortening in a skillet/stoneware pan and preheat to 400°. Mix ingredients. Pour in preheated pan and bake till done.

Vanessa Channell, Ringgold Primary School

In the late fifties, Peanut Faircloth (front) poses with his band (from left) Howell "Hal" Cullpepper, Charlie Evans, and Norman Blake.

Indian-Style Cornbread Fritters

1 1/3 cup of milk or 1 ¾ cup buttermilk
¼ cup olive oil
2 cups Aunt Jemima or Martha White self-rising cornmeal mix
1 large onion, finely chopped
2 large "dobs" peanut butter (if no one is allergic)

Mix ingredients well in bowl with pouring spout. Batter should be creamy and pourable. Pre-heat large non-stick frying pan on stove top. Pour batter in about 3-inch cookie size fritters. When fritters begin to look dry on top, flip with spatula. When good'n brown, take up. Stack on plate and stand back...You may wanta' taste-test the first two or three you take up, to get the hang of turning them at the right time. Practice with this will make it get better. Cover two or three of them on a plate, like pancakes, with honey, or maple syrup. If they turn out right, give a war-whoop and call in the tribe.

Charlie "Peanut" Faircloth CountryMusic Artist

Charlie "Peanut" Faircloth

Charlie "Peanut" Faircloth went toe to toe on the charts with Moon Mullican with his Decca recording "I'll

Faircloth

Sail My Ship Alone" in the early 1950s when the song hit the top of the country charts. Faircloth found early success doing live shows on the Mutual Radio Network from Macon, Georgia, when his "Mississippi River Blues" caught the ear of Ernest Tubb who helped him win a Decca recording contract. As a Georgia and Chattanooga radio and television personality, Faircloth helped many young performers, including Elvis Presley and Brenda Lee, gain attention. Faircloth currently performs with Curtis Hicks and the Old Time Strings. His Christmas song, "Reindeer Boogie," first recorded by Hank Snow, boogied again when Georgian Trisha Yearwood recorded it.

PRETESTING YOUR TASTEBUDS

Dot's Onion Cornbread

1 ½ cups cornmeal
¾ cup oil
2 eggs
1 small can cream style corn
1 small onion (chopped)
1-8oz container sour cream

Preheat oven to 400°. Combine ingredients in large bowl.
Heat pan or cast-iron skillet with about three tbsp butter.
Make sure sides of pan or skillet are well greased. Pour
remaining butter from pan into the cornbread mixture. Pour
mixture into pan or skillet and bake for 30-35 minutes or until
golden brown.

Darla Crawford
Learning Center Educational Coordinator

Farmers gather outside the Catoosa County
Agricultural Extension Service Agent's Office as rolls
of pine saplings await dispersal in the 1930s.

PRETESTING YOUR TASTEBUDS

Monkey Bread with Eggnog Glaze

2/3 cup water
2 eggs
¼ cup margarine or
butter, softened
3 ½ cups bread flour
1/3 cup sugar
1 tsp salt
1 tsp ground nutmeg
1 ½ tsp bread machine
yeast
Rum glaze (see below)
½ cup chopped pecans, if desired

Reading student Frances Holsinger (center) receives an award at the CCL banquet from Shirley Smith and Randall Franks.

Place all ingredients except rum glaze and pecans in bread machine pan in the order recommended by the manufacturer. Select dough/manual cycle. Grease 12-cup bundt cake pan. Prepare rum glaze (see below). Pour half of glaze into pan; sprinkle with ¼ cup of the pecans. Remove dough from pan, using lightly floured hands. Divide into 30 equal pieces; arrange in layers over glaze in pan. Pour remaining glaze over dough; sprinkle with remaining pecans. Cover and let rise in warm place about 45 minutes or until double. (Dough is ready if indentation remains when touched.) Heat oven to 350°. Bake 30 to 40 minutes or until golden brown. Let stand 5 minutes. Turn upside down onto serving plate; leave pan over bread 1 to 2 minutes to allow glaze to coat bread. Serve warm.

Rum Glaze

½ cup packed brown sugar
½ cup granulated sugar
1 cup whipping (heavy) cream
1 tsp rum extract

Mix all ingredients.

Frances Holsinger, Reading Student

PRETESTING YOUR TASTEBUDS

Praline Biscuits

½ cup butter (1 stick), cut into 12 pieces
½ cup light brown sugar, packed
36 pecan halves (I use pecan pieces)
cinnamon, to taste
2 cups Bisquick
1/3 cup applesauce
1/3 cup milk

Preheat oven 400 degrees. Arrange 1 piece of butter, 2 tsp of brown sugar and 3 of the pecan halves (I sprinkle in pecan pieces to cover the bottom) in each of 12 greased muffin cups. Sprinkle with cinnamon. Heat in oven until butter and sugar melt. Combine Bisquick, applesauce, cinnamon and milk in bowl. Stir for 20 strokes. Drop by spoonfuls over the butter mixture in the muffin cups. Bake about 10 minutes or until golden brown. Take knife or fork and gently loosen the sides of the biscuits. Invert onto serving platter immediately.

Vanessa Channell, Ringgold Primary School

"The main part of intellectual education is not the acquisition of facts but learning how to make facts live."

Oliver Wendell Holmes

PRETESTING YOUR TASTEBUDS

Riz Biscuits

1 cup buttermilk (warm)
1 pkg yeast
1 ½ tsp baking powder
½ tsp baking soda
2 ½ cups plain flour
2 tbsp sugar
4 tbsp shortening
1 tsp salt

Mix flour, salt, soda, and shortening. Dissolve yeast in buttermilk. Add flour mixture all at one time. If necessary, add more milk. Cut out and let rise one hour. Bake at 425°. Can be made earlier and kept in the refrigerator.

Donna Blevins, Head Start

The Civil War's Great Locomotive Chase, which occurred in April 1862 when Andrews' Raiders highjacked The General, came to an end just north of Ringgold on Ga. Hwy. 151.
(Photo by Randall Franks)

PRETESTING YOUR TASTEBUDS

Whisper Biscuits

1 pkg dry yeast
¼ cup warm water
3 cups all purpose flour
1 tsp baking powder
½ tsp baking soda
1 tsp salt
1 tbsp sugar
½ cup vegetable oil
1 cup buttermilk

Dissolve yeast in warm water, let stand 5 minutes. Combine flour and next 4 ingredients. Add yeast mixture, oil, and buttermilk. Stir until dry ingredients are moistened. Turn dough out onto a lightly floured surface. Roll to ½ inch thickness. Cut and place on ungreased baking sheet. Let rise in a warm place till doubled in thickness. Bake 400° for 15 minutes or till lightly browned. Dough can be refrigerated for 3 or 4 days before baking.

Bill Anderson
Singer/Songwriter

Bill Anderson

Georgia raised Country Music and Georgia Music Hall of Fame member Bill Anderson has more than 80 hits to his personal credit. Countless hits have come from his pen since his "City Lights" went to number one for Ray Price in 1958. Some of his personal hits include "Still," "Po Folks" and "Mama Sang a Song." In recent years, he has written or co-written hits for Vince Gill, Kenny Chesney, Mark Wills, Brad Paisley, Alison Kraus and George Strait. Anderson, who continues to star on the *Grand Ole Opry*, also appeared on the soap opera *One Life to Live* and hosted network game shows.
Visit www.billanderson.com.

PRETESTING YOUR TASTEBUDS

Yeast Rolls

1 cup whole milk
1 stick unsalted butter
8 oz water
4-5 cups King Arthur's unbleached bread flour
Or Gold Medal Better for Bread flour
1 ½ tsp salt
4 tsp Vital Wheat Gluten
1/3 cup sugar
2 (1/4 oz) pkgs Fleischmann's rapid rise yeast

Melt butter and warm liquids until temperature is between 85-110 degrees F. Using dough hook on mixer, mix 2 cups flour and remaining dry ingredients on medium speed until blended. Slowly add liquids and mix until well blended, scraping down sides if needed (about 2 minutes).

Add remaining 2 – 3 cups of flour, one cup at a time, until a soft dough forms, cleaning the sides of bowl but still sticking to bottom resulting in slightly sticky dough.

Place in lightly greased bowl, turning dough ball by hand a couple of times to grease the surface of dough. Place in a warm, draft-free area. Cover with towel and let rise until double in size. Punch down and place on floured surface. Shape into any desired roll type. Place in a very lightly greased (sprayed) pan. Let rise in warm place until double. Bake at 335 degrees until lightly brown.

For Pull-Apart Rolls:

Roll dough thin. Spread soft margarine lightly over surface of dough. Cut in about 1 ½ - 2 inch squares. Stack 4 squares together, with a non-margarine side on top & bottom. Place sideways in a very lightly greased (sprayed) muffin pan. Let rise in warm place until double. Bake at 335 for 20 minutes.

Vanessa Channell, Ringgold Primary School

SWEET RESULTS
(DESSERTS)

Catoosa Citizens for Literacy honors graduates

By Randall Franks

Families members and friends of all ages smiled, cheered and

applauded for the graduates' at the first Catoosa County GED (General Education Development) Graduation May 1, 2008 at the Colonnade, sponsored by the Catoosa Citizens for Literacy.

(Above) Graduates at the Catoosa County GED (General Education Development) Graduation May 1, 2008 at the Colonnade.
(Left) Mindy McCannon, Ph.D., Northwestern Technical College vice president of academic affairs, presents certificates to the graduates. "Education is something no one can take away from you....," she said. She encouraged the graduates to continue their work at the college using available state grants.

One of those being cheered was Benny Bankston, a retired pipe fitter and welder, but he was also among those applauding as his two daughters Noelie Bankston and Melissa McNabb also walked across the stage.

Bankston said his educational effort came from a desire that his daughter Noelie get her GED. Melissa achieved hers earlier and it became a friendly contest between the father and daughter to win the goal.

Since finishing her GED, Melissa went on to become a CNA and is working

Benny Bankston, and his two daughters Noelie Bankston and Melissa McNabb

to further her nursing education. Noelie said she wants to study to become a medical assistant.

When asked which of the family won the contest, Benny said, "We both won."

Approximately 200 people participated in the event that was followed by a reception at the Catoosa County Learning Center.

"In past years the GED graduation, held by Northwestern Technical College, was a joint effort which included all four surrounding counties," said Shirley Smith, Catoosa County Learning Center executive director. "This year each county conducted its own individual graduation. We were enthusiastic about the wonderful turnout for the event."

"We wanted to show our citizens how important it is to get an education," Smith said. "When those citizens, who have not had the opportunity to obtain a high school diploma or GED, see how GED graduates are received by our community leaders, I hope they will realize that completing their GED is and important goal that they should attain themselves."

"Our GED recipients will contribute greatly to the future of Catoosa County," Smith said.

Apple Crumble with Toasted-Oat Topping

6 medium apples
½ cup unsweetened apple-sauce
¾ cup old-fashioned or quick-cooking rolled oats
3 tbsp toasted wheat germ
3 tbsp packed light brown sugar
1 tsp ground cinnamon
1 tbsp canola oil
1 tbsp unsalted butter, cut into small pieces

Ritchie

Joanne Ritchie
CCL Taskforce member
Position: Volunteer tutor (non, low-level, and dyslexic readers)

How long have you served on the task force? Began in September 1997 on a part-time basis, but regularly participated the last four years.
Organizations: Rossville Church of Christ
Favorite Movie: Gone with the Wind
Favorite Book: Holy Bible
Philosophy: The Golden Rule – Do unto others as you would have them do unto you.
Why do you serve on the task force: I believe this ministry is what the Lord left me to do after surviving cancer.

Preheat oven to 350°. Coat a 12"x8" baking dish with non-stick cooking spray. Cut the apples in half, lengthwise. Remove the cores and stems and discard. Cut the apples into thin slices. Place the apples and the applesauce in the prepared baking dish. Toss to coat the apples evenly with the applesauce.

Spread out evenly in the baking dish. In a small bowl, mix the oats, wheat germ, brown sugar, and cinnamon. Drizzle with the oil. Add the butter. Mix with your fingers to work the oil and butter into the dry ingredients. Sprinkle the oat mixture evenly over the apples. Bake 30 to 35 minutes, or until the topping is golden and the apples are bubbling. Serve warm.

Joanne Ritchie, CCL Tutor

Apple Pie

Pastry for double-crust pie
¾ to 1 cup sugar
½ tsp cinnamon
¼ tsp salt
1 tsp grated lemon rind
2 tbsp flour
6 cups pared, sliced apples
1 tbsp lemon juice
2 tbsp butter

Smith

Combine sugar, cinnamon, salt, lemon rind and flour in mixing bowl. Arrange apples in layers in 9 inch pastry-lined pan, sprinkling cinnamon-sugar mixture over each layer. Sprinkle with lemon juice. Dot with butter. Roll out remaining dough. Cut slits for escape of steam. Moisten rim of bottom crust. Place top crust, pressing to seal. Flute edge. Bake at 450° for 10 minutes, then at 375° for 40 to 50 minutes, until apples are tender when pierced with fork. Serve with Crème Sauce.
Crème Sauce:

Combine 2 slightly beaten eggs, ¼ cup sugar and 2 tbsp lemon juice in saucepan. Cook, stirring constantly until thick.
Add 3-oz pkg softened cream cheese and ½ cup dairy sour cream.

Prepare apple pie, cutting a 1 ½ to 2 inch hole in center of top crust. Bake pie. Let stand 10 minutes. Pour crème sauce through opening. Cool completely. (For green apple pie, use 1 cup sugar and omit lemon rind and juice).
Scott & Melanie Smith, Northwest Georgia Bank

Denzel Washington

In *Remember the Titans*, two 1970s Virginia high schools were combined, forcing African American and white football players onto an integrated team. Denzel Washington's character, "Coach Herman Bone," helped to bring unity and teamwork to the team. The Academy Award® winner for supporting actor in *Glory* is one of Hollywood's top stars. His film credits include *Antwone Fisher*, *John Q*, *The Hurricane* and *The Preacher's Wife*.

Apple Surprise

1 can biscuits (10 count)
2 cups Mello-Yello
3-4 tart apples
1 stick butter
1 cup sugar
Cinnamon, to taste

Roll biscuits out in circle as you would for fried pies. Chop apples and sprinkle lightly with cinnamon and fold biscuit over. Place in baking dish that has been sprayed with cooking spray. Melt butter and add in sugar and Mello-Yello. Pour over biscuits and bake at 350° for 35-40 minutes.

Donna Blevins, Head Start

Aunt Mable's Brown Sugar Pie

1 cup brown sugar, packed
½ stick butter
3 tbsp milk or cream
1 egg
2 tbsp flour

Mix well and pour into an unbaked crust. Bake at 350° for 30 minutes.
Virginia Davis, mother of Donna Greeson

Bacardi ® Rum Cake

1 cup chopped pecans or walnuts
1 pkg (2 layer) yellow cake mix
1 pkg (4 serving size) Vanilla Instant Pudding and Pie Filling
4 eggs
½ cup cold water
½ cup vegetable oil
½ cup Bacardi dark rum (80 proof)

Sprinkle nuts evenly in bottom of greased and floured 10-inch tube or bundt pan. Combine cake mix, pudding mix, eggs, water, oil, and rum in a large mixing bowl*. Blend; then beat at medium speed for two minutes. Pour into pan. Bake at 350° for 60 minutes or until cake springs back when lightly pressed. Cool in pan 15 minutes. Remove cake from pan and prick with cake tester. Spoon warm Bacardi Rum Cake Glaze over warm cake.
*For high altitude areas, use large eggs, add ¼ all purpose flour, increase water to1 ¼ cups and reduce oil to ¼ cup; bake at 350° for 50 minutes.

Bacardi ® Rum Cake Glaze
1 cup sugar
½ cup butter or margarine
¼ cup water
½ cup Bacardi dark rum
Combine sugar, butter and water in saucepan. Bring to a boil; boil for 5 minutes, stirring constantly. Remove from heat. Stir in rum and bring just to a boil. Spoon glaze over warm Bacardi Rum Cake. Garnish if desired.

Linda Burnett

Baked Apples with Almonds and Raisins

4 small to medium apples, such
as Braeburn or Empire
1 tbsp melted butter, plus extra
to brush the apples and butter
the baking dish
1 heaping tbsp honey
pinch ground nutmeg
pinch ginger
2 pinches cinnamon
¼ cup raisins
1 tbsp almonds, toasted,
chopped, and blanched

(Photo: J. Miller)

Preheat oven to 400 degrees, and
butter a baking dish that is just
large enough to hold the apples.
Lightly toast almonds in a small dry
hot skillet and set aside in a small
bowl. Stem and core apples, but do
not cut through the bottom of the
apples. Using a small sharp knife,
score the circumference of each
apple, to prevent them from col-
lapsing while they bake. Combine
the remaining ingredients, and
using a small spoon stuff the filling
into the apples, tapping the filling
down firmly. Brush each apple with
melted butter, and place in baking
dish. Bake 30 to 40 minutes, until
apples feel soft when pierced with a
fork. Serve in individual dishes.
Pour a little of the syrup from the
baking dish on one side of the
apple, and a little heavy cream on
the other side.

Captain's Quarters Bed and Breakfast Inn

The Captain's Quarters,
on historic Barnhardt
Circle in Fort
Oglethorpe, is on the
National Register of
Historic Places. The residence was originally
built in 1902 as a duplex
for two cavalry captains
and their families. The
building was remodeled
in 1988 and served for
several years as a beau-
tifully decorated bed
and breakfast.

*Julie Powell, former owner of
Captain's Quarters Bed and Breakfast Inn*

Barbara Mandrell's Apple Cake

Serves: 4-6

3 tbsp butter or margarine
1 cup sugar
1 egg
1 cup flour
1 tsp baking soda
½ tsp cinnamon
½ tsp nutmeg
½ tsp salt
3 cups chopped apples
½ cup chopped pecans
1 tsp vanilla flavoring
Whipped cream or vanilla ice cream (optional)

(Photo: Exley)

Cream butter and sugar. Add egg and mix well. Stir together dry ingredients. Add to creamed mixture. Stir in apples, nuts and vanilla flavoring. Pour into a greased 8X10" pan. Bake at 350° for 45 minutes. While still warm, top with whipped cream or vanilla ice cream, if desired and serve.

Barbara Mandrell
Entertainer

Barbara Mandrell

Two-time Entertainer of the Year Barbara Mandrell was inducted into the Country Music Hall of Fame in 2009. With over 75 industry awards, she is one of the industry's best loved performers in history. People included her among their Beautiful at Any Age 2007-09. She and her sisters starred in the *Barbara Mandrell and the Mandrell Sisters* variety show on NBC. Visit www.barbara-mandrell.com.

77

Banana Split Cake

2 sleeves of graham
crackers
1 cup margarine, melted
& divided
1 box confectioners sugar
3 to 4 bananas
1 large can crushed
pineapple, drained
1-12 oz container non-
dairy whipped topping
1 pint strawberries or
cherries

Photo: Mike Morbeck

Make crust with graham
crackers mixed with ½ cup
melted margarine. Press
into bottom of 13x9 inch
cake pan. Whip confectioners sugar and ½ cup melted
margarine until fluffy.
Spread on top of crust.
Layer sliced bananas and
crushed pineapple. Top
with whipped topping. Put
strawberries or cherries on
top. Refrigerate. Serves 12

*David Davis of The
Warrior River Boys
Bluegrass Music Artist*

David Davis and the Warrior River Boys

Mandolinist David Davis continues a family tradition in performing Bluegrass. In the 1930s
his Uncle Cleo Davis joined
forces with mandolinist Bill
Monroe and created a style
of music that would change
popular music forever. In 1984
David Davis took over the
reins of the Warrior River Boys.
The band continues to thrill
audiences with their Rebel
Records release *Two Dimes
and a Nickel*. Members are
Marty Hays, Owen Saunders,
Daniel Grindstaff and Adam
Duke.   Visit
www.daviddavisandwrb.com.

Don't Touch My Butterscotch Pie

1 cup brown sugar
¼ cup cornstarch
½ tsp salt
Mix in saucepan and
gradually stir in:
1 cup water
1 2/3 cup milk
1/3 cup butter

Cook over medium heat, stirring constantly, until mixture thickens and boils. Boil 1 minute. Remove from heat and stir some of hot mixture into 3 egg yolks, slightly beaten. Then blend into the hot mixture in pan. Boil 1 more minute, stirring constantly. Remove from heat and blend in 1 ½ tsp vanilla. Pour into baked pie shell. Top with meringue and bake 8 to 10 minutes at 400° until lightly browned.

Jeannie Seely
Country Music Artist

Jeannie Seely

Grand Ole Opry star Jeannie Seely helped to re-shape the role of women in country music through a strong determination to turn her dreams into a reality. Through her dedication to her craft, in 1966 she won a GRAMMY® for "Don't Touch Me." In 1972, she penned the No. 1 song "Leavin' and Sayin' Goodbye" for Faron Young. After 13 consecutive years with songs on the charts, she continues to thrill audiences with new recordings, live performances and appearances in projects such as *Always, Patsy Cline,* Willie Nelson's *Honeysuckle Rose* and the film *Colored Eggs.* Visit www.jeannieseely.com.

79

Caramel Popcorn

1 cup butter
2 cups packed light
brown sugar
1 tsp salt
½ cup light corn syrup
1 tsp baking soda
5 bags of microwave
popcorn (butter flavor)

Heat oven to 200°. Pop
the corn and set aside. In
large sauce pan over
medium heat add the
first four ingredients.
Boil for five minutes and
remove from heat. Stir in
baking soda. Stir well.
Use large disposable alu-
minum pan and pour
mixture over popcorn
and mix making sure the
popcorn is coated well.
And be careful, sugar
mixture is very hot and
will burn you. Bake in
the oven at 200° for 1
hour taking it out every
15 minutes and stirring it
well. Pour it out on wax
paper and let it cool
completely before bag-
ging.

*Amy Carroll, Catoosa
County Health
Department*

Carroll

Amy Carroll

*CCL Task Force
member*

Position: County
Nurse Manager for
the Catoosa
County Health
Department

**Reason for serving on the Task
Force:** "We have
two programs at
the health depart-
ment through
which we refer
people to get their
GEDs."

**Organizations and
memberships:**
Pleasant Hill United Methodist
Church

Favorite movie: *Pretty Woman*

Favorite book: Any book by Lori
Wick

Favorite TV show: *Friends*

Favorite quote: "Do unto others
as you would have
them do unto you.

Philosophy: God did not give you
talents without
expecting you to
use them.

Cherry Chocolate Snack Cake

**1 Devil's Food cake mix
1 can cherry pie filling
6 regular sized Hershey
candy bars**

Preheat oven to 350°. Mix a packaged devil's food cake mix as directed. Fold in cherry pie filling. Bake at 350° until toothpick or knife inserted comes out clean. While cake is still hot, unwrap and place Hershey bars on top of cake. When candy bars are melted, spread them over the top of the cake. I like to use canned chocolate frosting for a more fluffy frosting.

*Donna Pierce,
GED Instructor*

Pierce

Donna Pierce
CCL Task Force Member
Position: Lead Adult Education Teacher

Why Literacy is important to me: Literacy is the key to a better life. It can help someone meet their family's needs for today, but it is so much more rewarding to help them learn skills to meet their needs for a lifetime.

Organizations and member ships: Catoosa Citizens for Literacy, Scholarship Committee

Favorite movie: *Gone with the Wind*

Favorite book: Whichever one I happen to be reading at the time.

Favorite TV show: *Jeopardy*

Favorite quote: This is the day which the Lord hath made; I will rejoice and be glad in it. *Psalm 118:24*

Philosophy: Keep smiling – Things have a way of working out for the better.

Chocolate Cobbler

½ cup margarine
1 cup sugar
2 cups flour, self rising
1 cup milk
¼ cup cocoa
Topping:
1 ½ cup sugar
1 ½ cup hot water
¼ cup cocoa

Cream sugar, cocoa and margarine. Add flour and milk. Pour in 13"x9" baking dish. Mix 1 ½ cup sugar and ¼ cup cocoa. Place on top of cake mixture. Pour 1 ½ cup hot water over top. Bake at 375° for 45 minutes.
Shirley Smith, Executive Director

The Kiwanis Club of Ringgold supports the Catoosa County Learning Center and other community programs through fundraisers such as its annual 1890s Day Jamboree Pancake Breakfast. Past President Peter Hanson (left) and members Jack Deaton and Jane Everett make up a few pancakes.

Chocolate Chip Ice Cream Pie

½ cup chocolate syrup
1/3 cup semisweet chocolate chips
2 cups crisp rice cereal
¼ cup sour cream
1 quart chocolate chip ice cream, softened

Coat bottom and sides of an 8-inch pie plate lightly with butter. Combine chocolate syrup and chocolate chips in a small microwave-safe bowl. Microwave on high power until hot about 45 seconds. Stir until smooth. Reserve ¼ cup of the chocolate mixture. Combine remaining chocolate mixture and cereal in a medium bowl and mix to coat cereal. Press mixture over bottom and up sides of prepared pie plate. Freeze until firm, about 15 minutes. Combine reserved chocolate mixture and the sour cream in a small bowl and mix well. Spread half the ice cream in the prepared pie plate. Drizzle with half the sour cream mixture. Top with remaining ice cream and drizzle with remaining sour cream mixture. Freeze pie, covered, until firm, about 1 hour.

Stacy Newton, Learning Center Childcare Provider

It is the supreme art of the teacher to awaken joy in creative expression and knowledge.

Albert Einstein

Ivy's Chocolate Pie with Meringue

1 cup milk
½ cup sugar (just a little over)
3 heaping tbsp cocoa
3 tbsp cornstarch
Dash of salt
3 egg yolks, beaten (reserve whites to make meringue)
1 tsp vanilla
1 tbsp butter
1 frozen or refrigerated pie crust

Beat egg yolk. Cook milk, sugar, cocoa, cornstarch and salt until thick stirring constantly. Add some of the hot mixture slowly to the eggs and then pour back into chocolate mixture. Cook until thick. Add vanilla and butter. Pour into pie crust. Top with meringue.

Meringue

3 egg whites at room temperature
1/3 cup sugar
¼ tsp cream of tartar
½ tsp vanilla

Beat egg whites, vanilla and cream of tartar until they form soft peaks. Slowly beat in sugar. Spread over pie. Be sure to seal the edges of the crust with the meringue. Bake at 350° for 15 minutes or until lightly browned.

Donna Blevins, Head Start

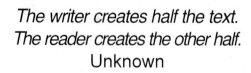

The writer creates half the text.
The reader creates the other half.
Unknown

Chocolate Strawberry Delight

24 chocolate flavored graham cracker squares (2 ½ inches each)
(makes approximately 2 cups chopped)
½ cup butter, melted
¼ cup sugar
12 oz Cool Whip
1 (3.9 oz) pkg instant chocolate pudding, not prepared
1 cup sour cream
1 pint strawberries, hulled & sliced
1 ounce semi-sweet chocolate, melted
2 tsp butter, melted

Finely chop graham crackers. Combine graham cracker crumbs, butter and sugar. Press into bottom and sides of round pan. Combine Cool Whip, pudding and sour cream with whisk. Pour half of filling over crust. Hull strawberries & slice. Layer strawberries on top of filling. Pour remaining filling over strawberries. Melt chocolate & butter together 1 minute 30 seconds on high; stir until smooth. Drizzle over top. Can grate additional chocolate over top. Sets immediately but can be refrigerated to chill.

Vanessa Channell, Ringgold Primary School

**"Education is the key to unlock the golden door of freedom."
George Washington Carver**

SWEET RESULTS

Cream Cheese Pound Cake

3 sticks pure butter, softened
1 large block cream cheese, softened
6 eggs
3 cups cake flour, sifted
3 cups white sugar
1 ½ tsp baking powder
1 tsp vanilla flavoring
1 tsp lemon flavoring

Cream together butter and cream cheese. Add eggs one at a time, beating after each addition. Add sugar one cup at a time. Beat well. Add sifted cake flour one cup at a time. Beating after each cup. Add baking powder and beat. Add flavorings and beat. Grease and flour a tube pan. Pour into pan and bake in a preheated oven at 300° for 60-65 minutes.

Mary Ruth Nichols

Through the Certified Literate Community Program (CLCP), locally owned collaboratives are changing their world, recognizing that education touches every aspect of life and community. CLCPs are living proof that citizens can be inspired to improve their individual lives while they make their communities better places to work and live. **Billie Izard**
Executive Director for Certified Literate Community Program

Citrus Crown Cake

1-12 oz jar orange marmalade
½ cup flake coconut
½ stick butter, melted
1 box Duncan Hines Moist Deluxe Lemon Supreme cake mix
3 eggs
1 1/3 cup water
1/3 cup oil

The Anchormen

Southern Gospel's Anchormen hit the top of the charts with their song "Giver of Life." The quartet of Keith Casstevens, Karl Rice, Michael Bartlett and Paul Harkey travels from Goldsboro, North Carolina, and takes the traditional quartet sounds to audiences around the country for more than 200 dates each year. Its last 15 radio singles have been in the national top #20 charts. Their song "I'll Meet You On The Mountain" was nominated in the top ten songs of the year for 2007. Visit www.theanchormen.com.

Preheat oven to 350°. Spray a 10-inch bundt pan with nonstick spray or grease and flour well. In a small bowl, combine marmalade, coconut, and melted butter. Pour into prepared pan. Prepare cake mix according to directions on box. Pour batter over marmalade mixture. Bake for 50-55 minutes. Remove from oven and cool in pan 10 minutes. Invert cake onto serving plate.

Anchormen
Southern Gospel Music Artists

87

Coca-Cola ® Cake

3 cups flour
2 cups sugar
2 sticks butter
1 cup Coca-Cola
1-1 ½ cups small marshmallows
½ tsp soda
½ cup buttermilk
1 tsp vanilla
3 tbsp cocoa
2 eggs, beaten

Combine sugar, flour and soda in mixing bowl. Heat the margarine, cocoa, and coca cola to boiling and mix well with sugar and flour mixture. Add milk, eggs, vanilla and marshmallows and mix well. Bake at 350° for 30-35 minutes in an oblong pan that has been greased and floured.

Icing

1 stick butter
6 tbsp Coca-Cola
1 box powdered sugar
3 tbsp cocoa
1 tsp vanilla
1 cup chopped pecans

Combine butter, Coca-Cola, and cocoa in saucepan. Heat to boiling. Pour over sugar. Add vanilla and beat on high speed two minutes. Add pecans and pour over hot cake.
Cool and cut in squares.

Wanda Guess

Covington 3-Day Coconut Cake

1 (18 oz.) box of Duncan Hines ®
Butter Cake Mix
2 cups powdered sugar
1 (16 oz.) container of sour cream
1 (12 oz.) container of frozen coconut
1 ½ cups frozen whipped topping
(Cool Whip ®)

Grady Spradley

Grady Spradley (left) and the late Carroll O'Connor pause on the set of *In the Heat of The Night* in the early 1990s. In addition to appearing in other movies, Spradley was O'Connor's

Mix cake mix according to directions and bake in round pans. When completely cool, split layers in half. To make the frosting, combine the powdered sugar, sour cream and coconut and blend well. Chill the frosting. Once chilled, reserve 1 cup of the frosting to use later. Spread the remainder of the frosting between the cooled cake layers and assemble the cake. Fold Cool Whip into the 1-cup of frosting. Blend until smooth. Spread on top and the sides of the cake. Seal cake in an airtight container (Tupperware container is ideal) for 3 days in the refrigerator before serving.

Grady Spradley Photo Double for Carroll O'Connor
In the Heat of the Night

89

Crockpot Apple Pie

8 tart apples, peeled and sliced (Granny Smith or Golden Delicious)
1 ¼ tsp ground cinnamon
¼ tsp allspice
¼ tsp nutmeg
¾ cup milk
2 tbsp butter, softened
¾ cup sugar
2 eggs
2 tsp vanilla
1 ½ cup Bisquick, divided
1/3 cup brown sugar
3 tbsp butter, cold
¼ cup raisins, optional
¼ cup walnuts, optional

Eveline Bryant
CCL Task Force Member
Position: GED Paraprofessional
Favorite movie: Lorenzo's Oil
Favorite book: Kaleidoscope by Danielle Steele
Favorite TV show: Criminal Minds
Favorite quote: "In this life we cannot do great things. We can only do small things with great love." Mother Teresa
Philosophy: If you smile at a person, 99 percent of the time they smile back.

Bryant

Toss apples in large bowl with cinnamon, allspice, and nutmeg. Place apple mixture in lightly greased slow cooker. Combine milk, softened butter, sugar, eggs, vanilla, and ½ cup of Bisquick. Spoon over apples. Combine the remaining bisquick with the brown sugar. Cut cold butter into bisquick mixture until crumbly. Sprinkle this mixture over top of apple mixture. Cover and cook on low 6 to 7 hours or until apples are soft. Serve with large scoop of vanilla ice cream.

Eveline Bryant, GED Paraprofessional

Dump Cake

1 can (16oz) crushed pineapple
1 can (16oz) cherry pie filling
1 box yellow cake mix
½ cup margarine
½ - 1 cup pecans

Layer pineapple, cherry pie filling, dry cake mix, and pecans in a greased 13x9-inch pan. Top with slices or strips of the margarine. Bake at 350° for 50 minutes or until top is lightly browned.

Joy Thornton

EARLY RINGGOLD SHOPPING

In the early 1900's, one choice for Catoosa County shoppers was McClain's on Nashville Street. Owned by Joe McClain (center), the store was located at the current site of "My Favorite Things" antiques. "They had groceries and men's shoes, but they did not have ladies shoes. Back halfway through the store, they had feed and fertilizer — anything and everything that the farmer needed," said Mary Lynn Clark, who was just a girl when her father R.L. Magill (right) went to work at McClain's. "I remember we would empty up a 100-pound bag of sugar into these big containers; then we would fill up the brown paper bags with five pounds and 10 pounds of sugar." Clark related that Gus Jay (left) and her father went out of their way many times to help customers.
(Photo from George Hendrix Collection)

SWEET RESULTS

"Dixie Hoedown" Strawberry Shortcake

3 cups sifted all-purpose flour
4 ½ tsp baking powder
2 tbsp sugar (if desired)
1 ½ tsp of salt
¾ cup of shortening
1 cup milk
2 quarts fresh strawberries, hulled, cut in quarters, and sweetened
Butter
Half and half
Whipped cream

Photo: Joy McReynolds

Jesse McReynolds

IBMA Hall of Fame member and *Grand Ole Opry* star Jesse McReynolds innovative mandolin style set a standard for generations. He tours and hosts events at the Pick Inn at his Gallatin, Tenn. home. For more than 50 years stars Jim & Jesse McReynolds and the Virginia Boys pushed the envelope of Bluegrass with releases such as *Berry Pickin' Time in the Country*, a 1960s album featuring all Chuck Berry material. At the same time, the act set a standard for a smooth bluegrass and country sound. The duo received the National Heritage Fellowship Award from the National Endowment for the Arts. Visit www.jimandjesse.com.

Sift the dry ingredients together and cut in the shortening. Add the milk and mix to soft dough.
Knead lightly for 20 seconds. Divide the dough in half. Put ½ into a greased 9-inch layer pan. Spread a thin coating of shortening over the dough in the pan and cover with the rest of the dough, patting to fit pan. Bake at 425 degrees for 30 minutes. Separate the layers. Spread the bottom layer with butter and cover with ½ of the strawberries. Place the upper layer on top of the berries and cover with the remaining strawberries. Pour a little milk (preferably half-and-half) over the shortcake and serve topped with whipped cream. Makes 10 to 12 servings.

Jesse McReynolds and the Virginia Boys

Dom DeLuise

SWEET RESULTS

Dom's Death by Chocolate

For cooks who are being watched!

2 cups flour
1 tbsp double-acting baking powder
½ tsp baking soda
2 cups sugar
3 large eggs
1 stick unsalted butter at room temperature
1 cup sour cream
½ cup Seagram's Godiva Liqueur
2 tsp vanilla extract
½ cup + 2 tbsp cocoa
1 pkg (12oz) semisweet chocolate chips
Powdered sugar
1 bundt pan

Sift flour, baking powder and baking soda twice. Place in a small bowl. Beat the sugar and eggs in a large mixing bowl until sugar is dissolved. Add butter and mix into egg mixture thoroughly. Add sour cream, liqueur, vanilla extract and beat. Add flour mixture and cocoa and beat slowly just until flour is absorbed. Do not overbeat. Fold in chocolate chips and pour into buttered bundt pan. Bake at 350° for 1 hour. When cool, sift powdered sugar on top.

Dom Deluise, Actor/Comedian

Dom DeLuise

The late Dom DeLuise (1933-2009) kept America laughing throughout his careers on stage, television and theater screens. From his days on the *Garry Moore Show*, *The Entertainers*, *The Dean Martin Show* to his own series *Dom DeLuise and Friends*, television audiences laughed at his antics. He provided tremendous comedic performances in films such as *Smokey and the Bandit II*, *Cannonball Run I and II*, the Mel Brooks films *Blazing Saddles* and *History of the World - Part I* and many others. Food also was a big part of the performer's life, as he became a respected Cookbook author, chef, and kitchen products entrepreneur. He even was a best selling children's book author and a favorite voice for numerous animated movie characters such as "Tigar" in *An American Tail*, and "Itchy" in *All Dogs Go to Heaven I and II*.
Visit
www.DomDeLuise.com.

Eight Egg Cake

8 eggs
2 cups self-rising flour
2 cups sugar
1 cup oil
vanilla flavoring
Beat eggs 6 minutes on high speed, add sugar and oil mix
well. Add flour and flavoring. Beat 7 minutes on high speed.
Pour into greased tube pan and bake at 325° until toothpick is
inserted into cake and comes out clean.
Nelson & Marie Richardson, Southern Surveying

Johnnie Sue and Friends on the set of their former
UCTV3 TV Show in 2005. From left, the late Jimmie
Rodgers, Robert Taylor, Nelson Richardson, Joe
Rodgers and Johnnie Sue. All of the performers
were inducted into the North Georgia Musicians Hall
of Fame on display at Park Place Restaurant in Fort
Oglethorpe in 2008 and 2009. (Photo by Randall Franks)

Marie Hammock's Easy Fruit Cobbler

1 can fruit pie filling (any flavor)
1-6 slices white bread
1 stick margarine, melted
¾ cup sugar
1 egg

Use 8x8 pan. Pour in pie filling. Cut bread into finger strips and place over fruit, close together. Fill in spaces. Add sugar and beaten egg to the melted margarine, mix well and pour over the bread. Bake at 350° for 40-45 minutes.

Donna Blevins, Head Start

Ralph Emery

Ralph Emery once visited nightly with cable viewers through his TNN show *Nashville Now*. Viewers often referred to him as the Johnny Carson of country music. This was simply how more TV viewers came to know this talent who chronicled the ups and downs of careers of the biggest stars in the industry for decades on radio and television. He became the most famous TV and radio personality in country music and he was inducted in 2007 to the Country Music Hall of Fame ®.

Visit TheNashvilleShow.com.

Fabulous Cheesecake

3 pkg cream cheese
1 cup and 3 tbsp sugar, divided
1 tbsp and 1 tsp vanilla
3 eggs
1 tbsp lemon juice
1 ½ cups graham cracker crumbs
½ cup margarine, melted
1 pint sour cream

To make crust, mix margarine, ½ cup sugar, and the graham cracker crumbs. Press into casserole dish or spring form pan. Bake at 350° for five minutes. For the filling, mix cream cheese, ½ cup sugar, vanilla, eggs one at a time, and lemon juice. Pour over crust. Bake at 350° for 25 minutes. For the topping, mix together sour cream, 3 tbsp sugar, and 1 tsp vanilla. Pour over the baked cream cheese. Bake an additional five minutes. Let cool and refrigerate.

Grace Davis, Parent Involvement Coordinator, Catoosa County Schools

Shortly after his marriage in 1916, Former President Dwight David Eishenhower and his bride Mamie were stationed at Fort Oglethorpe, Georgia in the fall of 1917.
(Photo courtesy of the Dwight David Eishenhower Presidential Library)

French Coconut Pie

3 eggs
1 ½ cups sugar
1 cup coconut
2 tbsp cornmeal
2 tbsp cream
1 tbsp vinegar
½ stick butter, melted
1/8 tsp salt
1 tsp vanilla

Add ingredients to melted butter and mix well. Pour into unbaked 9 inch pie shell. Bake in 325° oven until pie is set in the middle. Cool and serve.

"I have enjoyed reading so much since I was a small child, so it just comes naturally to me to want to share the ability to read with adults who cannot read. It gave me such joy recently when one of my students told me that this was the first time that she ever got to go and choose, without help, a Valentine for her husband. When adults learn to read, it increases their self-confidence and seems to give them a whole new outlook on life. The goal of one of my students was simply to be able to read the Bible, but when she finished the course of reading, she then wanted to go on and get her GED so that she could get the job she desired. To touch the lives of adults who cannot read means so much that I cannot understand why there aren't more who want to do this."

Joan Jolley
Reading Tutor

Egg Custard Pie

4 eggs
1 ½ cup sugar
½ cup self-rising flour
2 cups whole milk
1 stick margarine, melted
1 tsp vanilla

Beat together eggs, sugar and flour...add one at a time. Stir in the milk, melted margarine, and vanilla. Beat on high with electric mixer. Spray 10-11 inch pie plate with Pam. Bake at 350° for 50 minutes.

U.S. Congressman Nathan Deal

U.S. Congressman Nathan Deal

Congressman Nathan Deal has served what is now the 10th Congressional District of Georgia since 1992. Having grown up as the son of two school teachers and then married to a teacher, the Sandersville, Georgia, native feels right at home working on education and other issues of concern to Catoosa County residents as well as all his constituents. Congressman Deal attended and spoke at the opening of the Shirley Smith Learning Center, Catoosa County's adult learning center and the home base of the literacy program for the county. He is running for Governor of Georgia for 2010.

German Chocolate Upside-Down Cake

1 box German choco-
late cake mix + ingredi-
ents according to box
1 cup chopped pecans
1 small can coconut
8 oz cream cheese, soft-
ened
1 box powdered sugar
1 tsp vanilla
2 sticks butter, melted

Mix powdered sugar,
cream cheese, butter, and
vanilla until creamy and
smooth. Set aside.
Grease 9x13 pan. Cover
with pecans and then
sprinkle coconut over
pecans. Make cake mix
according to directions
on box. Pour over the
pecan/coconuts. Spoon
cream cheese mixture
over cake mix. Bake at
350 for 55 minutes.

Vanessa Channell

Dolly Parton

Like "Shine" (her 2001 GRAM-MY® award-winning song), Dolly Parton's work shines to brighten the world. Her recordings include "I Will Always Love You" and "Here You Come Again." Among her films for the big and little screen are *9 to 5* and *Blue Valley Songbird*. After decades of hit songs and films, she still finds time through her Dollywood Foundation to support education and improve the quality of life for all children in Sevier County, Tennessee. Begun in Sevier County to provide preschoolers with a book each month from birth until kindergarten, the Foundation's *Imagination Library* has spread to 800 communities in 41 states. With the help of local sponsors, the foundation gives away five million books each year. Visit www.dollypartonmusic.net.

Dolly Parton and her husband Carl Dean were married at the First Baptist Church of Ringgold in Catoosa County. Ga. on May 30, 1966.

Islands in the Stream

3 eggs, sepa-
rated
2/3 cup sugar
2 heaping tsp
flour
1 quart milk
1 tsp vanilla
nutmeg,
optional

Cream egg
yolks with
sugar and whip
until smooth,
add flour and
mix well.
Scald the milk,
and when hot
enough, add the cream mixture. Stir constantly 20 to 25
minutes until it thickens, remove from heat and add
vanilla. Boil some water. Whip egg whites and add to
water until hardened. Remove with spatula and put on
top of the cream mixture. Sprinkle with nutmeg. Chill.

Dolly Parton, Country Music Artist/Actress

"It'll be Joy" Mound Pie

This is a family recipe (Grandmother) used for special Holiday get-togethers! It's actually more of a cookie or candy than a pie. Hope you enjoy it as much as we do!

CRUST

1 stick softened butter or margarine
1 cup crushed graham crackers or vanilla wafers

Blend well, then press into the bottom and sides of an 8"x 8" x 2" glass baking dish.

PIE FILLING

1 cup Angel Flake coconut
1 cup chopped pecans
1 cup chocolate chips (or 1/2 cup chocolate chips & 1/2 cup peanut butter chips)
1 can Eagle Brand milk

Layer one ingredient at a time - first coconut, then pecans, next chocolate chips and finally, pour the Eagle Brand Milk over the top. Bake at 350 degrees for 30 minutes.

Phil Cross
Southern Gospel Singer

Phil Cross

For more than two decades, Southern Gospel singer and composer Phil Cross has found that "The Key" (one of his five No. 1 songs) in ministry is to *Turn to the One*. The winner of the Dove Award for songwriting in 1989 for "Champion of Love" is a native of Ringgold, Georgia. Cross won his second Southern Gospel Music Association's Songwriter of the Year Award in 2002. After eleven years of guiding his highly acclaimed quartet, The Poet Voices, Cross decided to pursue a solo career including his love of choral music. His latest CD is entitled *The First 25 Years*. Visit www.philcrossmusic.com

Homemade Ice Cream

1 ½ pint half & half
1 ½ cup sugar
2 tbsp + 1 1/8 tsp vanilla
5 eggs
½ tsp salt
¾ can Eagle Brand
9 cups milk

Do not use less than ¾ can of Eagle Brand and no more than 1 can. If mixture is too sweet, add 1 cup milk to cut sweetness.

For Pineapple Ice Cream
18 oz Pineapple preserves
15 oz crushed sweet pineapple

For Strawberry Ice Cream
Add 3 cups fresh or frozen strawberries.

Wanda Guess

Holcombe

Melissa Holcombe
CCL Taskforce member
Position: Social Worker/Homeless Liaison, Catoosa County Schools
Reason for serving on task force: The ability to read is fundamental to success in life.
Favorite Movie: *Midnight in the Garden of Good and Evil*
Favorite Author: Michael Connelly
Favorite TV Show: *Boston Legal*
Favorite Quote: "In this life we cannot do great things. We can only do small things with great love." – Mother Theresa
Philosophy: I cannot help everyone, but I can help someone

Jam Raisin Cake

1 ½ cups self-rising flour
1 cup sugar
1 cup blackberry jam (seeded or seedless)
½ tsp cinnamon
3 eggs
1 cup butter (no margarine)
3 tbsp cocoa
½ cup raisins
1 cup buttermilk
1 tsp nutmeg
1 tsp vanilla
½ cup nuts
Pinch of soda

Mix all ingredients except raisins and nuts, mix well. Add raisins and nuts. Bake at 350° for 30 minutes.

Wanda Guess

Smiley Burnette

R.L. McNew added this photo of cowboy sidekick Smiley Burnette visiting Ringgold in 1959 to the George Hendrix collection. Burnette, who starred in more than 125 films with stars like Gene Autry, Roy Rogers and Sunset Carson and co-starred in *Petticoat Junction*, was in Catoosa County to celebrate the opening of the new location of McNew Pharmacy on Lafayette Street. "We had a soda fountain and served sandwiches," pharmacist R.L. McNew said in 2003. "We had the things you would find in most independent pharmacies." McNew remembered there was a huge crowd to see Burnette, who composed more than 300 songs and is in the Nashville Songwriters' Hall of Fame. "He did two shows right in front of our building. We filled up the street; everybody wanted to see Smiley," McNew said. McNew, daughter Pam (right) and (from left) restaurant owner Leon Richardson and the Shop-Rite grocery store manager (name unknown) visit with film star Smiley Burnette. (Photo from George Hendrix Collection)

Kool-Aid Pie

1 can Eagle Brand milk
1 large cool whip
2 pkgs Kool-aid, any flavor
2 graham cracker pie crusts
Mix Eagle Brand milk and Kool-Aid together. Fold in cool
whip. Pour into pie crusts. Refrigerate immediately. Chill well.
Serve and Enjoy!

Karen Austin, Learning Center Childcare Provider

While Tunnel Hill proper lies within Whitfield County, areas of
the community lie within the borders of Catoosa County. The
Tunnel Hill Historical Foundation operates a historical center at
the pre-Civil War railroad tunnel and an annual Battle of
Tunnel Hill Re-enactment occurs each year.
(Photo courtesy of Bradley Putnam)

Japanese Fruit Cake

2 cups sugar
1 cup butter
4 eggs
2 tsp baking powder
1 cup milk
3 ¼ cups flour
Dash salt
1 tsp vanilla

Cream butter and sugar. Add eggs and beat well. Add dry ingredients alternately with milk. Mix only until combined. Divide batter- to ½ add:

1 lb raisins
1 tsp cinnamon
½ tsp cloves

Bake in two separate layers at 350° for 25 minutes or until cake tests done. Cool on rack.

Filling:
2 cups sugar
1 grated fresh coconut
1 cup boiling water
Juice of two oranges or lemon

Mix together and add 1 cup flour and juice of coconut and cook until thick and done. Put filling between layers and then cover the top of cake. Cake is better the next day. Should be refrigerated.

This is a traditional family recipe. My dad had to have a Japanese Fruit Cake every year at Christmas and any other time he could talk someone into making one. It is a depression type cake and involves several steps but it really is worth the trouble.
Jane Scroggins

Lemon Chess Pie

2 cups sugar
1 tbsp all purpose flour
1 tbsp cornmeal
¼ tsp salt
¼ cup butter or margarine, melted
2 tsp grated lemon rind
¼ cup lemon juice
¼ cup milk
4 eggs
1 unbaked 9-inch pastry shell
1 cup heavy cream, chilled
2 tbsp sugar

Combine sugar, flour, cornmeal, and salt. Add butter, lemon rind, lemon juice, and milk; mix well. Add eggs, one at a time, beating well with a wire whisk after each addition. Pour into pastry shell. Bake at 350° for 50 minutes. Yield: 1 (9 inch) pie. Beat heavy cream with sugar to soft peaks. Serve this as a topping for pie. Optional: A little bourbon can be added to cream.

Shirley Carver-Miller
Former First Lady of Georgia

Shirley Carver-Miller

During the time she served as Georgia's First Lady, Shirley Miller made it her challenge to change the face of illiteracy in Georgia. She succeeded in that challenge working along with her husband, Governor Zell Miller. By the end of the Miller administration, adult literacy teachers were working in every county in the state; an adult literacy enrollment of 90,000 students annually had been achieved; and more than 22,000 GED diplomas were being awarded each year.

107

Lib's Fudgy Chocolate Pie

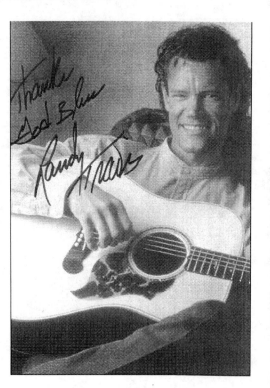

1- 9-inch unbaked
pastry shell
1- 4 oz pkg sweet
cooking chocolate
¼ cup butter or mar-
garine
1- 14 oz can Eagle
Brand sweetened
condensed milk
2 eggs, slightly beat-
en
½ cup hot water
1 tsp vanilla extract
1/8 tsp salt
½ cup chopped
pecans
1 cup flaked coconut

Preheat oven to 350°. In heavy saucepan, over low heat, melt
chocolate and margarine; remove from heat. In large mixer
bowl, combine sweetened condensed milk and warm chocolate mixture. Mix well. Stir in eggs, hot water, vanilla, and
salt. Mix well. Pour into shell. Top with pecans and coconut.
Bake for 35 to 40 minutes or until coconut is lightly browned.
Serve warm or chilled. Refrigerate leftovers. Makes one 9-
inch pie.

Randy Travis
Country Music Artist/Actor

Randy Travis

Traditional country hit maker Randy Travis finds himself as much at home on the movie set as in the recording studio. In addition to guest appearances on TV's *Matlock*, *Touched by an Angel*, and *Texas*, he has numerous films among his credits. Some are *The Rainmaker* starring Jon Voight, Matt Damon and Danny DeVito, *Frank and Jessie* with Bill Paxton and Rob Lowe, *Black Dog*, with Patrick Swayze, *Fire Down Below* with Steven Seagal and *White River Kid* with Antonio Banderas, Ellen Barkin, Lily Tomlin and Bob Hoskins. Travis filmed a starring role in *Texas Rangers* with James Van Der Beek, Dylan McDermott and Usher. He starred in *The Wager* with Jude Ciccolella, Nancy Stafford, and Bronson Pinchot in 2008. His *Around the Bend* CD received a Dove Award for Best Country Album in 2009. Songs from *Inspirational Journey* inspired a two-part season finale of the CBS-TV series *Touched by an Angel* in which Travis also appeared.
Visit
www.randytravis.com.

Louisiana Chocolate Spice Cake

2 cups all purpose flour
2 cups granulated sugar
1 tsp baking soda
1 tsp ground cinnamon, optional
¼ tsp salt
¾ cup hot water
2 sticks margarine
¼ cup unsweetened cocoa
½ cup buttermilk
1 tsp vanilla extract
2 large eggs

Preheat oven to 375°. Prepare 13x9 baking pan with cooking spray and coat with 2 tsp flour. Combine 2 cups flour and next four ingredients in a large bowl. Stir well with a whisk. Combine water, margarine and ¼ cup cocoa in a small saucepan, bring to boil, stirring frequently. Remove from heat; pour into flour mix. Beat with a mixer at medium speed until well blended. Add buttermilk, 1 tsp vanilla, and eggs; beat well. Pour batter into prepared pan. Bake at 375° for 22 minutes or until a wooden pick inserted in center comes out clean.

Continued next page

Louisiana Chocolate Spice Cake Icing:

1 stick margarine
6 tbsp milk
4 tbsp unsweetened cocoa
1 box powdered sugar
¼ cup pecans, chopped
2 tsp vanilla extract

Combine margarine milk and cocoa in a medium saucepan. Bring to boil, stirring constantly. Remove from heat, and gradually stir in powdered sugar, pecans and 2 tsp vanilla. Spread over hot cake. Cool completely.

Evans

Brenda Evans
CCL Task Force member
Position: Manager, Occupational Wellness, Hutcheson Medical Center
Reason for Serving on the taskforce:
A community that has a focus on literacy is one that plans, anticipates and expects a successful workforce.
Organizations and Memberships:
Walker and Catoosa County Chambers of Commerce
Favorite Movie: *Marley & Me* and *Fire Proof*
Favorite TV Show: *Reba* and *Army Wives*
Philosophy:
Live for today because you can't change yesterday and tomorrow may never come.

Grace York, mother of Shirley Smith, Executive Director

"If you can read this, thank a teacher."

Anonymous

Lite Coconut Cake with Lite Buttercream Frosting

Serves: 16
Cake:
Cooking spray
1 tbsp cake flour
2 ½ cups cake flour (about 10 oz)
2 tsp baking powder
½ tsp salt
2 cups sugar
6 tbsp butter, softened
¼ cup egg substitute
2 large eggs
¾ cup light coconut milk
¼ tsp coconut extract
Frosting:
1 cup sugar
¼ cup water
5 large egg whites
½ tsp cream of tartar
1/8 tsp salt
¼ cup butter, softened
¼ tsp coconut extract
3 tbsp toasted, flaked, sweetened coconut

Preheat oven to 350°. To prepare cake, coat 3 (8 inch) round cake pans with cooking

Peters

Nancy Peters

Charter Member of the Task Force
Position: Manager of Student Accident Insurance
Business: Weeks and Peters Insurance
Reason for Serving on the taskforce: To help bring the joy of reading and learning to others.
Organizations and Memberships: Charter member of Catoosa Citizens for Literacy, Catoosa Schools' Partnership 2000, Ringgold First Baptist Church
Favorite Movie: Most current is "Australia"
Favorite Book: Mystery novels, Detective Novels by Ian Rankin, books by Patricia Cornwell and Sue Grafton
Favorite TV show: HGTV design and gardening shows and Food Network
Favorite Quote: "Every time a child is born, it brings with it the hope that God is not yet disappointed with man..." Rabrindranath Tagore
Philosophy: "Do unto others as you would have them do unto you."

spray; line bottoms of pans with wax paper. Lightly coat wax paper with cooking spray; dust pans with 1 tbsp flour. Lightly spoon 2 ½ cups flour into dry measuring cups, and level with a knife. Combine flour, baking powder, and salt, stirring with a whisk. Place 2 cups sugar and 6 tbsp butter in large bowl; beat with a mixer at medium speed for 2 minutes or until well blended. Add egg substitute and eggs to sugar mixture; beat well. Add flour mixture and coconut milk alternately to sugar mixture, beginning and ending with flour mixture. Stir in ¼ tsp extract. Spoon batter into prepared pans. Sharply tap the pans once on countertop to remove air bubbles. Bake at 350° for 25 minutes or until a wooden pick inserted in the center comes out clean. Cool in pans 10 minutes on wire racks; remove from pans. Remove wax paper; discard. Cool cakes on wire racks. To prepare frosting, combine 1 cup sugar and ¼ cup water in a saucepan; bring to a boil. Cook 3 minutes, without stirring, or until a candy thermometer registers 250°. Combine egg whites, cream of tartar, and 1/8 tsp salt in a large bowl; using clean, dry beaters, beat with a mixer at high speed until foamy. Pour hot sugar syrup in a thin stream over egg whites, beating at high speed until stiff peaks form, about 3 minutes. Reduce mixer speed to low; continue beating until egg white mixture cools (about 12 minutes).
Beat ¼ cup butter until light and fluffy; stir in ¼ tsp extract. Fold in 1 cup egg white mixture. Fold butter mixture into remaining egg white mixture, stirring until smooth. Place 1 cake layer on plate; spread with 1 cup frosting. Repeat twice with cake layers and 1 cup frosting ending with cake layer; spread remaining frosting over top and sides of cake. Sprinkle with toasted coconut. Chill until set.

Nancy Peters, Weeks and Peters Insurance

Microwave Peanut Butter Fudge Candy

½ cup butter or margarine
2 cups sugar
½ cup unsweetened cocoa
1/8 tsp salt
½ cup milk
3 cups quick-cooking rolled oats
½ cup shredded or flaked coconut
½ cup chopped peanuts or other nuts
½ cup peanut butter
2 tsp vanilla

In mixing bowl, melt butter in microwave for 45 seconds. Add sugar, cocoa, salt and milk; blend well. Cook uncovered for 5 minutes stirring once. Stir in remaining ingredients. Pour into greased 12x7 or 13x9 inch pan. Cool several hours at room temperature or in refrigerator; Cut into squares. Tips: To make individual candies, drop by teaspoonful onto wax paper. This candy freezes well. To thaw quickly arrange several pieces on plate and heat about 15 seconds.

Todd Smith

Ringgold's Evans House at Guyler and Nashville streets in Ringgold served as a boarding house during the Civil War where nurses Fannie Beers and Kate Cumming boarded during their service in Confederate hospitals. The privately-owned site is part of the Chickamauga Campaign Trail.
(Photo by Randall Franks)

Nancy Reagan's Brownies

3 squares semi-sweet baking chocolate
3 sticks butter
2 cups granulated sugar
1 ½ tsp salt
1 tbsp vanilla
2 squares unsweetened baking chocolate
6 eggs
2/3 cup cake flour
1 tsp baking powder
2 cups finely chopped pecans
Confectioner's sugar

Melt chocolate and butter in top of double-boiler, then cool. Beat eggs, add sugar until light in color. Add chocolate mixture to egg mixture. Sift together flour, salt, baking powder: add to other ingredients. Mix in vanilla and nuts. Pour into buttered, floured 12 by 18 inch pan. Bake in preheated 350° oven for 30 to 35 minutes. Cool, cut, then sprinkle with confectioners' sugar.

Nancy Reagan
Former First Lady of the United States
of the United States

Nancy Reagan

Former first Lady Nancy Reagan helped to enlighten Americans and the world about problems with substance abuse as she encouraged youth to "Just Say No." She said drug abuse knows no boundaries; it crosses all lines—geographical, racial, political and economic. In 1994 the Nancy Reagan Foundation and BEST Foundation for A Drug-Free Tomorrow developed the Nancy Reagan Afterschool Program. A former MGM actress, she starred in eleven films. Among them are *The Dr. and the Girl*, *East Side/West Side*, *Shadow on the Wall*, *The Next Voice You Hear*, *Night into Morning*, *It's a Big Country*, *Shadow in the Sky*, *Talk About a Stranger*, *Donovan's Brain* and *Rescue at Sea*. In her 1957 film, *Hellcats of the Navy*, she co-starred with her husband Ronald Reagan, future President of the United States. She has written two books including her memoirs, *My Turn*, and *I Love You, Ronnie*.

Story Musgrave
GED recipient

Before Astronaut Story Musgrave, M.D., was able to touch the heavens in six space flights he first had to begin his journey by getting his GED after leaving the Marines.
According to Musgrave, receiving his GED opened the door to further education. He earned the NASA Distinguished Service Medal in 1992. One of Musgrave's hobbies is reading.

Mississippi Mud Cake

1 ½ cups all-purpose flour
4 eggs
1 cup pecans, chopped
½ cup cocoa
1 can (3 ½ oz) coconut
1/8 tsp salt
1 cup butter, melted
1 jar (7 oz) marshmallow cream
2 cups sugar

In bowl, mix the flour, nuts and coconut. Set aside. Combine butter, sugar, eggs, cocoa and salt in a large mixing bowl. Add flour mixture and mix well. Pour into greased and floured 9x13 pan. Bake 350 degrees for 30-35 minutes and immediately spread marshmallow cream over the cake.

Cool. Spread frosting after cooled. Note: can use mini marshmallows instead of marshmallow cream. Also, the cake can be prepared in advance and refrigerated until ready to serve.

Continued next page

Mississippi Mud Cake Frosting:

1 box powdered sugar
½ cup butter, melted
1/3 cup cocoa
1/3 cup evaporated milk
¼ tsp vanilla
1 cup pecans, chopped (optional)
Combine all ingredients in large bowl. Spread over cooled cake.

Vanessa Channell, Ringgold Primary School

The Battle of Ringgold Gap

On Nov. 27, 1863, Confederate Brig. Gen. Patrick Cleburne and his men stood fast at Ringgold Gap to prevent Federal troops from passing through. Many tourists stop by the Ringgold Gap Battlefield tourism area south of Ringgold on U.S. 41 where a bronze statue of Cleburne will be unveiled in October 2009 thanks to Ringgold Telephone Co. Patrick Cleburne Society and the city of Ringgold.
(Photo by Randall Franks)

RINGGOLD GAP
November 27, 1863

After the Battle of Missionary Ridge, Bragg's Confederate Army retreated in disorder toward Dalton. Brig. Gen. Patrick R. Cleburne was ordered to take position in the gap, hold back the Federals, and save the trains and artillery from capture.
Exercising his only independent command, Cleburne utilized the terrain and his well-trained troops to hold up Federal pursuit for five precious hours. The trains and artillery were saved. By Joint Resolution the Confederate Congress thanked Cleburne for his achievement.

GEORGIA HISTORIC MARKER
029-16

Mom's Cherry Cake

1½ cups butter
2 cups granulated sugar
4 eggs
1 tsp each: vanilla, almond and lemon extract
4 cups all-purpose flour
2 tsp baking powder
1 tsp salt
1 cup milk
1 ½ cups each: halved red and green candied cherries

With electric mixer, cream butter with sugar thoroughly. Add eggs, one at a time, beating well after each. Beat in extracts. Combine 3 ½ cups of flour with baking powder and salt; mix thoroughly. Add flour mixture to creamed mixture alternately with milk. Toss cherries with remaining ½ cup flour; fold into batter. Pour into well-greased and floured 10-inch bundt pan. Bake in 325° F oven for 1 hour and 45 minutes or until tester inserted in center comes out clean. Let cool a few minutes in pan, then turn out onto a wire rack to cool completely.

Anne Murray
Country Music Artist

Anne Murray

One of the most unique performers in the world, Anne Murray of Canada continues to amass gold and platinum awards for her albums. After 34 years of performing, her most recent gold and platinum achievements came with the release of CDs *Country Croonin'* and *What A Wonderful World*. Murray, the first inductee into the Canadian Association of Broadcasters' Hall of Fame, made her first hit with "Snowbird" in 1970. She has received four GRAMMY® awards, three American Music Awards, three Country Music Association Awards, three Canadian Country Music Association Awards, thirty-one Juno Awards and an induction into the Juno Hall of Fame in 1993. She has her own star at Hollywood and Vine and another on Canada's Walk of Fame on King Street in Toronto. Her 2007 CD *Duets* pairs her with top female performers sharing some of her greatest performances. Her autobiography *All of Me* was released in October 2009.

118

Buck Owens

As a child, the late Buck Owens (1929-2006) and his family plowed their way out of the dust bowl of Texas and moved to Arizona where he eventually dropped out of school to earn a living. With his guitar and voice, he created a new sound for country music in the 1960s and 70s. All he had to do was "Act Naturally" (his first major hit), catch "A Tiger by the Tail" and ride it all the way to the "Streets of Bakersfield" (his 1988 duet performed with Dwight Yoakam). This media mogul, who plowed his way to the top, owned radio stations and weekly publications. Visit www.buckowens.com.

Mother Owens' Banana Pudding

1 cup sugar
3 tbsp flour
½ tsp salt
2 eggs
2 ½ cups milk
2 tsp vanilla
1 small box vanilla wafers
4 large bananas, sliced

Combine sugar flour and salt in pan. Add eggs to milk and then add this mixture to the sugar-flour mixture and blend. Cook over medium heat, stirring constantly, until thickened. Add vanilla and remove from heat. Line bottom of bowl or pan with vanilla wafers, then put a layer of sliced bananas over the wafers. Pour part of the cooked custard over these two layers. Repeat another set of layers of wafers-banana-custard, ending with custard mixture, and sprinkle with wafer crumbs. Refrigerate until well chilled.

Buck Owens
Country Music Artist

119

My Mom's Oatmeal Cake

1 cup oatmeal
1 cup hot water
1 box of brown sugar
½ cup shortening
3 eggs
1 cup flour
1 tsp nutmeg
1 tsp cinnamon
1 tsp baking soda
powdered sugar, optional

Mix the oatmeal and hot water together and set aside. Mix all other ingredients together and blend thoroughly. Blend together with oatmeal. Pour into 8-inch pan (spray pan so cake will not stick) and bake for 30 minutes at 350°. Check center for doneness. Cool completely and sprinkle with powdered sugar (optional).

"Literacy unlocks the chains of ignorance. Literacy, and the will to use it, expands the logic, imagination, and success of those who take advantage of it."

Johnny Counterfit
Comedian

Johnny Counterfit

Country comedian Johnny Counterfit brings a unique cast of characters wherever he goes. Whether imitating Archie and Edith Bunker or Johnny Cash or when showing former President Bill Clinton and former First Lady Hillary Clinton how the President really sounded at the White House, Counterfit brings laughter and music to every performance. His first big break came on *America's Funniest People*. The Silver Microphone Award winner added his talents to create the voice of Rex in the Disney Channel's Emmy® winning *Claymation Christmas Celebration.*
Visit www.johnnycounterfit.com.

SWEET RESULTS

Mom's Apple Cobbler

½ cup butter or margarine
2 cups sugar
2 cups water
1 ½ cups self-rising flour (Martha White)
½ cup shortening
1/3 cup milk
2 cups apples, finely chopped
1 tsp cinnamon

Heat oven to 350°. Melt butter in a 13x9x2 inch baking dish or sheet cake pan. In a saucepan, heat sugar and water until sugar melts. Cut shortening into flour until particles are like fine crumbs. Add milk and stir with a fork only until dough leaves the side of the bowl. Turn out only lightly floured board or pastry cloth. Knead just until smooth. Roll dough out into a large rectangle about ¼ inch thick. Sprinkle cinnamon over apples; then sprinkle apples evenly over dough. Roll up dough like a jelly roll. Dampen the edge of the dough with a little water and seal. Slice dough into about 16 slices, ½ inch thick. Place in pan with melted butter. Pour sugar syrup carefully around rolls. (This looks like too much liquid, but the crust will absorb it.) Bake for 55-60 minutes. Makes 8 servings.

Viola Keith, Aunt of Shirley Smith

"I find television very educating. Every time somebody turns on the set, I go into the other room and read a book."

Groucho Marx

Mouth Watering Bread Pudding

6 to 7 slices of stale bread
1 egg beaten
½ cup honey
pint of half & half
½ pint heavy cream
1 stick of butter
dash ground nutmeg
2 tsp vanilla extract
fresh grapes (yes, that's correct)

Pyrex dish with cover. Pan, large enough to hold Pyrex dish with water in it. Preheat oven to 450°. In a sauce pan, place half & half, butter, heavy cream and honey. Slowly heat until warm. Stir in nutmeg, vanilla extract, and beaten egg. Butter inside Pyrex dish. Tear bread into bite-size pieces. Layer bread, then layer grapes, ending with layer of bread on top. Pour mixture over bread/grapes (should wet all of the bread, if not, add a little milk). Cover dish, place in the pan of water. Place in oven at 450° for 10 minutes. Lower heat to 350° and cook for 35 to 40 minutes. Great hot or cold.

Bill Cosby, Actor

Bill Cosby
(GED recipient)

The Cosby Show set the tone for 1980s sitcoms. Portraying "Dr. Cliff Huxtable," Bill Cosby instilled the values of education in his son "Theo" and his other children. Cosby left high school before finishing. He received his GED while serving in the Navy and now holds a Ph.D. In the 1960s, the stand-up-comedian-turned-actor opened doors for African Americans when he landed a starring role in *I Spy*, winning three Emmy © awards. Through his performances, albums and numerous television shows, including the popular children's cartoon *Fat Albert and the Cosby Kids*, he has made audiences laugh and taught children and adults life lessons. Cosby continues to pursue various facets of entertainment. This TV Hall of Fame member has encouraged millions to stay in school through his comedy, acting, producing, writing and hosting TV and radio. He and his wife Camille support educational efforts across the country. Visit www.billcosby.com.

Photo: Erinn

Norma Moore

In 1957 Norma Moore played Mary Piersall opposite Anthony Perkins' character in *Fear Strikes Out* (The Jimmy Piersall Story), and in 1958 she starred in the film *Unwed Mother*. Her credits include appearances on numerous classic television shows such as *Have Gun Will Travel* and *Perry Mason*. In the 1980s and 90s, Moore returned to the screen, landing roles in *Problem Child*, *Born on the Fourth of July* and *Walker, Texas Ranger*.

Nutty Buddy Pie

3 chocolate pie crusts
8 oz cream cheese*
½ cup skim milk
2 cup confectioner's sugar
2/3 cup crunchy peanut butter
2-8oz cool whip*
Hershey's syrup
Chopped pecans

(*cream cheese and cool whip may be "Lite" and still be delicious)
Combine cream cheese with milk. Add peanut butter, confectioners sugar, and fold in Cool Whip. Pour into pie crusts. Decorate with drizzled chocolate syrup and chopped nuts. Freeze until ready to serve. Leftovers can be re-frozen until used.

"There is nothing more important than reading. The world opens to you with reading because education is the equalizer between rich and poor. And without reading, there is no education!"

Norma Moore
Actress

Oatmeal Chocolate Chip Peanut Butter Coconut Crisps

1 ½ cup butter
1 cup peanut butter
2 cups sugar
2 cups brown sugar
2 tsp vanilla
5 eggs
3 cups sifted all-purpose flour
2 tsp salt
2 tsp baking soda
6 cups quick oats
2 cups coconut
12 oz chocolate chips
Preheat oven to 350°. Cream together butter, peanut butter, and both sugars until fluffy and smooth. Stir in vanilla and add eggs one at a time mixing well after each addition. Combine flour, salt, baking soda, oats, coconut, and chocolate chips. Mix well. Add to creamed mixture. Drop by spoonfuls on to greased cookie sheet. Bake for 10 to 15 minutes.

Richard and Cheryl McCrumb
Georgia Northwestern Technical College Student

Oreo Balls

1 pkg Oreo cookies, crushed
8 oz cream cheese, softened
1 pkg white almond bark
1 pkg chocolate almond bark (optional)

Using a blender or hand held mixer, mix Oreos and cream cheese together. Roll into walnut size balls. Chill for an hour. Melt approximately 3/4 package of white almond bark. Stick a toothpick in an Oreo ball and dip it in the melted white almond bark. Allow to harden on wax paper. This process takes about 15 minutes. While waiting, melt about 1/4 package of chocolate almond bark. When Oreo balls are no longer sticky to the touch, decorate with drizzles of chocolate and white almond bark.

Vanessa Channell, Ringgold Primary School

Former First Lady Laura Bush

Former First Lady Laura Bush was both an elementary school teacher and a librarian. Early reading, literacy and early childhood development programs, are among the biggest issues that she advocated for throughout President George W. Bush's time as Texas governor and in the White House. She introduced the National Book Festival in Washington, D.C. modeled after one she created in Texas. She initiated the "Ready to Read, Ready to Learn" highlighting the importance of reading aloud to and with children from their earliest days.

Peach Cream Pie

5-6 cups sliced peaches (sweetened to taste)
3 well-beaten eggs
1 cup sugar
1 cup heavy cream
2 unbaked pie crusts

Fill 2 unbaked pie crusts with sliced peaches (sweetened to taste). Mix together 3 well-beaten eggs, 1 cup sugar, and 1 cup heavy cream. Pour over peaches. Bake 15 minutes at 400 degrees. Reduce heat to 350° and bake 30 minutes.

Laura Bush
Former First Lady of the United States

Peanut Butter Fudge

¾ cup peanut
butter
¼ cup milk
1 box powdered
sugar
¼ cup butter

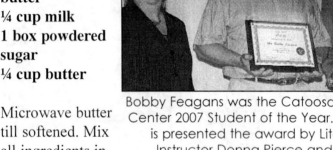

Bobby Feagans was the Catoosa Learning Center 2007 Student of the Year. Feagans is presented the award by Literacy Instructor Donna Pierce and CCL chairman Randall Franks

Microwave butter till softened. Mix all ingredients in a large glass bowl. Microwave for 2 minutes. Stir well & put into small buttered dish. Refrigerate & cut into squares.
Vanessa Channell, Ringgold Primary School

Peanut Butter Pie

1 large block cream cheese, softened
¾ cup confectioners sugar
1 cup peanut butter
2 tbsp milk
1 (8oz) whipped topping
1 graham cracker crust

Beat cream cheese and confectioners sugar together. Add peanut butter and milk. Fold in whipped topping. Pour into graham cracker crust and chill for several hours. Serve with additional whipped topping if desired. Simple, Easy & Delicious!
David Austin, Computer Instructor

Peanut Butter Ice Cream

1 cup creamy peanut butter
2/3 cup granulated sugar
1 cup whole milk
2 cups heavy cream
1 ½ tsp vanilla extract

This recipe is for a 1.5 quart ice cream maker
In a medium bowl, combine the creamy peanut butter and
sugar with an electric hand mixer and beat until smooth. Add
the milk and blend on low speed for about 2 minutes until the
mixture is smooth and the sugar has been dissolved. Stir in the
heavy cream and vanilla with a mixing spoon or a whisk.
Cover with plastic wrap and chill in the refrigerator for 2
hours. When ready, pour the ice cream base into your frozen
ice cream maker bowl. Let mix until thickened, about 15-20
minutes. If you are adding in candies or peanuts, add them in
the last 5 minutes of mixing. Pour into a freezer safe container
and freeze for at least 2 hours. Enjoy your ice cream topped
with dark chocolate or milk chocolate ice cream toppings.

Grace Davis, Parent Involvement Coordinator,
Catoosa County Schools

There are many little ways to enlarge your child's world. Love of books is the best of all.

Jacqueline Kennedy

Peanut Butter Pumpkins

1 box powdered sugar
12 oz peanut butter
1 tsp vanilla
1 stick melted butter
Drops of red & yellow food coloring (to make desired orange color)

Combine all above ingredients**. Roll into small balls & score with a toothpick to make pumpkin look. Top with a chocolate chip
**may have to add a few drops of water

Vanessa Channell, Ringgold Primary School

Peanut Pie

4 oz cream cheese
1 cup confectioner's sugar
½ cup creamy peanut butter
½ cup milk
9 oz cool whip
1 graham cracker crust (9"), baked and cooled.
¼ cup finely chopped salted peanuts

Whip cheese until soft and fluffy. Beat in sugar and peanut butter. Slowly add milk, blending thoroughly. Fold topping into mixture. Pour into baked pie shells. Sprinkle with chopped peanuts. Freeze until firm and serve.

Roberta Boyd

Quick Apple Crisp

5 Granny Smith apples (about 6 cups)
1/4 cup butter or margarine, melted
1/2 cup nuts, chopped (optional)
1 pkg (9 ounces) yellow cake mix
2 tbsp sugar
1 tbsp cinnamon
Vanilla ice cream or thawed, frozen whipped topping
(optional)

Preheat oven to 350°F. Peel, core and slice apples. Cut apples
in half crosswise. Place apples in a deep dish baker or pie
plate. Microwave butter on HIGH 60 seconds or until melted.
Chop nuts. Add nuts, cake mix, sugar and cinnamon to bowl;
mix until crumbly. Sprinkle mixture evenly over apples. Bake
35-40 minutes or until apples are tender and topping is golden
brown. Serve warm with ice cream, or whipped topping, if
desired.

Vanessa Channell, Ringgold Primary School

The film *Keep Your Powder Dry*, starring Lana Turner, Laraine Day and Susan Peters, and featuring a story line about the Women's Auxiliary Army Corps, was filmed on location at the Post in Fort Oglethorpe in 1945. Beginning in 1943 the post served as a training camp for more than 5,000 women.

(Photos courtesy 6th Cavalry Museum)

Real World Red Velvet Cake

 lan Jackson

Cake:
2 1/2 cups of plain flour
1 1/2 cups of sugar
1 1/2 cups of Wesson oil
2 eggs
1 cup of buttermilk
1 tsp of vanilla
1 tsp of baking soda
1 tbsp of cocoa
1 tsp of white vinegar
1oz bottle of red food coloring
Pinch of salt

Mix all ingredients at once until smooth. Grease and flour baking pans (one 9 x 13 rectangular pan or two 9 inch pans). Bake at 350° for approximately 30 minutes.

Icing:
1 1/2 boxes of powered sugar
12oz of cream cheese (softened)
1 1/2 cups of chopped pecans
1 1/2 sticks of margarine
1 tsp of vanilla

Blend together all ingredients except pecans until smooth and creamy. Mix in pecans.
ICE THE CAKE & ENJOY!

Alan Jackson
Country Music Artist

Georgia Music Hall of Fame member Alan Jackson has sold over 50 million albums worldwide since his *Here In The Real World* debut in 1989. The Newnan, Georgia, native reminisces about lessons passed from father to son in his song "Drive (For Daddy Gene)." As a songwriter he has penned many stories of the modern-day South. Jackson touched the hearts of millions with his 29th career No. 1 song, "Where Were You? (When the World Stopped Turning)," written following the tragic events of September 11, 2001. His latest Gold CD is *Good Time.* He has 34 No. 1 songs and is the most nominated artist in CMA history. Visit www.alanjackson.com.

Scripture Cake

3 ½ cups I Kings 4:22 - flour

1 cup Judges 5:25 - butter

2 cups Jeremiah 6:20 - sugar

2 cups I Samuel 30:12 - raisins

2 cups Nahum 3:12 - figs

2 cups Numbers 17:8 – almonds (chopped fine)

½ cup Judges 4:19 - milk

2 tbsp I Samuel 14:25 - honey

2 tsp Amos 4:5 - baking powder

Season to taste with II Chronicles - spice

A pinch of Leviticus 2:13 - salt

Six of Jeremiah 17:11 - eggs

I use 1 Tbsp each of allspice, cinnamon and nutmeg

Croft

Paul Croft

Charter Member of the Task Force

Position: Dupont Retiree

Reason for serving on the Task Force: To assist others in learning and to prepare them for the job market.

Organizations and Memberships: Member of Mt. Peria Baptist Church, Ringgold Kiwanis

Favorite movie: Men of Honor

Favorite book: Bible

Favorite TV show: CNN

Favorite quote: What will be different tomorrow because I am here today?

Philosophy: Thou shalt love thy neighbor as thyself.

This is a fun cake to make, but also a very delicious one if the directions are followed. Cream together the butter and sugar until light and very fluffy. Add sifted flour, baking powder, salt and spices alternately with the milk and the honey. Dredge raisins and figs in a very small amount of flour and stir in with the almonds. Pour into a large greased and floured tube pan. Bake at 350° for 1 hour and 30 minutes or until tests done.

Recipe by: Jo Pearl Adams

Paul Croft, Catoosa Citizens for Literacy Task Force Member

Joe Diffie

Before reaching "Home," his 1990 first No. 1 song, Joe Diffie spent time learning and honing his craft. He credits Bluegrass with helping him to learn harmony; and after moving to Nashville, he learned his writing skill by working with other top songwriters. The *Grand Ole Opry* Star, who also enjoys reading, credits his family for starting it all as he found his chart-topping success in country music. His latest release is *The Ultimate Collection*. Visit www.joediffie.com.

So Help Me Red Velvet Cake

2 eggs

1 ½ cups Wesson oil

1 ½ cups sugar with 1 tsp cocoa

2 ½ cups flour with ½ tsp salt

1 cup buttermilk w/ 1 tsp soda

1 tsp vinegar

1 tsp vanilla

2 oz red food coloring

Mix together all ingredients and bake at 350° for 30 minutes until tested done. Let cool.

Icing:

1 box powdered sugar

½ stick oleo

8 oz cream cheese (let soften)

1 tsp vanilla

1 ½ cups chopped pecans

Mix ingredients, add nuts and spread evenly over cake.

Joe Diffie, Country Music Artist

Marie D. Barnes and Former Governor Roy Barnes

As Honorary Chair for The Georgia Early Learning Initiative, former Georgia First Lady Marie Barnes traveled throughout the state reading to children and talking with parents about the importance of reading to young children. Mrs. Barnes stressed to parents of young children the important role that reading plays in quality early childhood education. She also helped create the State

Advisory Committee on Universal Newborn Hearing Screening. In 1999, Governor Roy Barnes signed legislation requiring that all babies born in Georgia hospitals be screened for hearing loss before they are discharged from hospitals.

Spud Dobbs Apricot Cake

2 cups oil
4 cups sugar
6 eggs
2 tsp ground cloves
2 tsp cinnamon
4 cups self-rising flour
3 – 6 oz jars apricot baby food
2 cups chopped pecans

Preheat oven to 300°. Grease 4 loaf pans. Mix first 7 ingredients, beat at medium speed until blended. Add nuts, mix. Pour into prepared pans, bake 50-60 minutes. Remove from oven, let stand 10 minutes. Unmold onto a sheet of heavy duty foil. Mix 1 cup fresh lemon juice with 2 ½ cups confectioners sugar. Drizzle it slowly over cakes allowing it to soak in.

Marie D. and Roy Barnes, Former First Lady and Governor of Georgia

Strawberry Cream Pie

1- 8oz pkg cream cheese
¼ cup granulated sugar
½ tsp vanilla
dash of nutmeg
1 cup strawberry slices
1 cup whipping cream
¼ cup sifted confectioner's sugar
1- 9-inch graham cracker pie crust

Combine softened cream cheese, granulated sugar, vanilla and nutmeg, mixing until well blended. Mash ¾ cup strawberry slices; stir into cream cheese mixture. Whip cream with confectioner's sugar until stiff peaks form; fold into cream cheese mixture. Fold remaining strawberries into cream cheese mixture. Spoon into crust. Chill several hours or overnight. Garnish with additional strawberries.

Shirley Wheeler for
The Marksmen

The Marksmen Quartet

Beginning their travels for Jesus in 1967 as a Southern Gospel quartet, music of The Marksmen Quartet eventually began to reflect the sounds that emanated from the hills and the "hollers" of their North Georgia mountain home near Murrayville, Georgia. For many years, fathers and sons Earle and Mark Wheeler and Keith and Darrin Chambers made up the quartet. Keith Chambers retired in 2002. One of Bluegrass music's top gospel groups, Earle and Mark Wheeler, Darrin Chambers, Davey Waller and Mark Autry cross into many genres and reaching millions. They are four-time Contemporary Bluegrass Gospel Group of the Year and Country Gospel Quartet of the Year. Visit www.marksmen-quartet.com.

Super Low-Cal Strawberry Shortcakes

2 quarts of fresh strawberries
1 large box of sugar-free
Strawberry Banana Jell-O
12 ready made shortcakes
1 pint of Lite Cool Whip
topping

Stem, wash, drain, then halve the strawberries. Set aside in large mixing bowl. Prepare (as directed on box) the Sugar-free jello…*but use only one cup of hot water. Mix the gelatin well, stirring until the gelatin is only lukewarm and beginning to thicken. Add the fresh strawberries and gently mix for approximately three minutes. Spoon generously over each shortcake and top with a large dollop of Lite Cool Whip topping. Serve Immediately…and enjoy! This recipe will serve approximately 12 people. *Calories per normal servings will equal less than 150. Fat content is zero for gelatin and berries…but dependent upon the type of shortcake you use.

Linda Dotson-Wooley
for Sheb Wooley Actor/Music
Artist

Sheb Wooley

From 1959-67, the late Sheb Wooley (1921-2003) rode into America's living rooms as Pete Nolan on *Rawhide* alongside Clint Eastwood. From classic film appearances in *High Noon* with Gary Cooper and *Giant* with James Dean, Wooley blazed a trail in American cinema that will never be erased. In 1986, Wooley played principal Cletus Summers in the Gene Hackman film *Hoosiers*. In the film, Cletus Summers instilled that while anybody can make a mistake, everyone should be given another chance. Including his self-penned hit *The Purple People Eater*, Wooley garnered several million-selling songs under his name and as his alter ego, Ben Colder. Visit www.shebwooley.com.

Ree Ree's Chocolate Icing

2 squares chocolate
6 tbsp butter
1 ¾ cup sugar
1 tbsp corn syrup
½ tsp salt
1 tsp vanilla
½ cup evaporated milk

Put everything in a boiler and stir until everything melts. Bring to a boil and boil hard for two minutes. Use to ice a yellow cake. Ice cake while the icing is still warm. Icing will thicken and harden to a fudge-like consistency as it cools.

Donna Blevins, Head Start

The Georgia monument at Chickamauga Battlefield
(Photo by Randall Franks)

138

Triple-Layer Mud Pie

3 squares semi-sweet chocolate, melted
1/4 cup canned sweetened condensed milk
1 chocolate pie crust (6oz)
1/2 cup chopped pecans, toasted*
2 cups cold 2% milk
2 pkg (3.9 oz each) chocolate instant
pudding
1 tub (8oz) whipped
topping, thawed, divided

Mix chocolate and condensed milk; pour into crust. Sprinkle with nuts. Beat milk and pudding mixes with whisk 2 minutes; spoon 1-1/2 cups over nuts. Stir ½ whipped topping into remaining pudding; spread over pudding layer in crust. Top with remaining whipped topping. Refrigerate 3 hours.
*to toast pecans – preheat oven to 350°. Spread pecans in single layer in shallow baking pan. Bake 5-7 minutes or until lightly toasted, stirring occasionally.

Nancy Peters

Before The Everly Brothers were hitting the charts singing "Bye, Bye Love" and "Wake Up Little Susie," Rock 'n' Roll Hall-of-Famer Don Everly rode over the Tennessee State line and married Sue Ingraham in Ringgold.

Three Minute Chocolate Mug Cake

One large coffee mug
4 tbsp plain flour
4 tbsp sugar
2 tbsp baking cocoa
1 egg
3 tbsp milk
3 tbsp oil
3 tbsp chocolate chips (optional)
Small splash vanilla

Combine dry ingredients in large mug and mix well. Add the egg and mix thoroughly. Pour in the milk and oil and mix well. Add the chocolate chips and vanilla, and mix again. Put your mug in the microwave and cook for three minutes at 1000 watts. The cake will rise over the top of the mug, but don't bealarmed. Allow to cool a little and tip out onto a plate if desired.

Linda Burnett

Barney Miller (center) on stage at Ringgold's Colonnade Theater for the play "An Appalachian Gathering" for the Share America Foundation, Inc.
Musicians are Ronal Graham (left) and Jerry Burke (right).

World's Best Coconut Pie

½ stick mar-garine, melted
3 large eggs, beat-en
1 cup sugar
¼ cup buttermilk
1 tsp vanilla
1 cup coconut

Mix ingredients and pour into 9" unbaked pie shell. Bake at 350° for 40 minutes.

Mary and Barney Miller, Country Music Musician

Barney Miller

Barney Miller (center) is one of country music's premier steel and dobro players. In 1957, he and Capt. Bill Durham (left) were on the road with in San Juan with country star Claude Casey (right). Miller began his performance career traveling in the late 40's with western sidekicks Dub Taylor and Al "Fuzzy" St. John. Miller has also performed and recorded with country stars such as late *Grand Ole Opry* star Billy Walker, entertainer Randall Franks, Bailey Jester, among others.

Brooks and Dunn

Since a *Brand New Man* hit the charts, Kix Brooks and Ronnie Dunn, multiple-time Entertainers of the Year, have become one of the most awarded country music duos in history. They have sold 30 million albums and scored 23 No. 1 hits and have won over 80 major industry awards. Their latest project is *Cowboy Town*. Visit www.brooks-dunn.com.

Reading, Writing & Arithmetic...

The

Main Course

(Meats & Main Dishes)

The annual 1890s Day Jamboree, held each Memorial Day weekend in Ringgold, draws thousands to enjoy gospel music, a fiddle contest, arts and crafts, food, a parade, kiddie rides and fun for the whole family.
Caleb Bryant (left) of Northport, Ala. won the ages 10 and under category in the 1890s Day Jamboree Fiddle Contest in 2009. (Photo by Randall Franks)

1890s Day Jamboree in Ringgold

Award Winning Crock-Pot Chicken and Dressing

3 chicken breasts with skin
Celery leaves
1 cup chopped onion
1 cup chopped celery
¼ cup oil
¾ tbsp salt
1 tbsp sage, or to taste
1 tsp poultry seasoning, or to taste
2 cups day-old white bread, broken into pieces
8 cups cornbread
2 cans cream of chicken soup
2 cans chicken broth, (better to use broth from chicken breasts)
3 eggs
1 tbsp apple cider vinegar

Rossville resident Merrie Lynn Youngblood won *Good Morning America* and Emeril Lagasse's Slow Cooker Challenge receiving a trip to New York and a Gold Slow Cooker in March 2009.

Put chicken breasts in water to cover, add a few celery leaves, pinch salt and pepper. Cook until chicken is tender. May do the night before and refrigerate overnight.

Sauté the onion and celery until tender in ¼ cup oil; add salt, sage, and poultry seasonings. Combine the breads in a large mixing bowl; stir in the onion/celery mixture. In a small bowl, combine the soup, broth, eggs and vinegar; mix well. Combine with the other ingredients in the large bowl. Mix well. Pour into crock pot that has been sprayed with oil; cook on high for 30 minutes. Turn heat to low and cook 3 ½ hours.

Remove skin from chicken and break chicken into large pieces, then fold into dressing. Cook dressing about 1 hour longer or until it starts to brown.

Merrie Lynn Youngblood

Balsamic-Plum Glazed Pork Chops

1 tsp butter
4 – 4oz boneless center-cut loin pork chops (about ½ inch thick)
¾ tsp salt divided
¼ tsp freshly ground black pepper
Cooking spray
2 tbsp chopped shallots
1 tsp bottled minced garlic
¼ cup port wine
2 tbsp balsamic vinegar
1/3 cup plum preserves
Chopped fresh parsley, optional

Melt butter in a large nonstick skillet over medium-high heat. Sprinkle pork evenly with ½ tsp salt and pepper. Add pork to pan; cook 3 ½ minutes on each side. Remove from pan. Coat pan with cooking spray. Add shallots and garlic to pan; sauté 30 seconds. Add port wine and vinegar to pan; cook 30 seconds, stirring occasionally. Stir in remaining ¼ tsp salt and plum preserves; cook for 30 seconds or until smooth, stirring constantly. Return pork to pan; cook 30 seconds or until desired degree of doneness, turning to coat. Sprinkle with parsley, if desired. Couscous and green beans complete the meal.

Nancy Peters

"Not all readers are leaders, but all leaders are readers."

Harry S. Truman

Basic Quiche

6 eggs
1 cup heavy cream
Salt, to taste
Pepper, to taste
1 cup grated cheese

Preheat oven to 350°. Beat eggs with cream, salt and pepper. Add cheese and mix well. Pour into buttered quiche or round cake pan. Bake 40 minutes or until golden brown. Optional: add ½ cup crisp bacon, diced ham, turkey, etc.
Vanessa Channell, Ringgold Primary School

Bow Tie Pasta with Italian Sausage

1 package Italian Mild Sausage Links
1 package (1 lb) bow tie pasta
1 tbsp olive oil
1 can of diced tomatoes
½ cup of diced onion
2 garlic cloves, minced
1 cup heavy whipping cream
½ cup of chopped fresh parsley
Parmesan cheese to taste
If you like things spicy add some red pepper flakes
Remove sausage from casing and cook with onion and olive oil until brown in a large skillet; add garlic right before the meat is done. Just allow the garlic to soften. Meanwhile, cook pasta according to package directions. Add the tomatoes and cream to the sausage mixture. Cook for about five minutes. Drain pasta; add to sausage mixture. Toss to combine. Sprinkle with fresh parsley and parmesan cheese. Serve immediately with some crusty bread.
Jill Van Dyke, Catoosa County Health Department

Chicken and Bean Slaw Wraps

2 (6 oz) pkgs fully cooked chicken strips, chopped (or left-over chicken)
1 ½ cups coleslaw mix with carrots
1 can (15 oz) chili powder-seasoned pinto beans, drained (or chili w/ beans)
1/3 cup Ranch dressing
½ cup chopped green onions
8 (8 inch) flour tortillas
1 cup (4 oz) shredded Cheddar cheese
½ cup BBQ sauce (I like KC Masterpiece)

Combine first five ingredients and set aside. Place tortillas on baking sheets and sprinkle evenly with cheese. Bake tortillas at 350° for 3-5 minutes, until cheese is melted. Top tortillas evenly with chicken mixture. Drizzle with BBQ sauce. Roll up in jelly-roll fashion (to help them stay rolled up, can wrap in plastic wrap, twisting ends of plastic to seal). Cut in half. Serve immediately.

Vanessa Channell, Ringgold Primary School

Christa Plank was the Catoosa Learning Center 2008 Student of the Year. Plank is presented the award by Literacy Instructor Donna Pierce and CCL co-chairman Knox Farmer

148

Jett Williams

Country singer Jett Williams and the Drifting Cowboys entertain audiences around the world. Their work incorporates a blend that includes her original songs from her CD *I'm So Lonesome I Could Cry* and such country classics as "Your Cheatin' Heart" and "Jambalaya" made famous by her late father, country legend Hank Williams. The story of Jett Williams' efforts to prove her real identity as Hank Williams' daughter became the best-selling autobiography *Ain't Nothin' As Sweet As My Baby*. Her latest CD is *Honk*. Visit www.jettwilliams.com

BBQ Deer

Medium Deer Roast
1 clove garlic
1 medium onion
1 tsp liquid smoke
Dash of Tabasco
BBQ sauce
½ tsp crushed red pepper
Salt & pepper, to taste

Boil roast until tender with garlic and onion. Drain and shred (remove any fat). Add liquid smoke, Tabasco, red pepper, salt and pepper, and barbecue sauce. Preheat oven to 350º. Bake for 15 to 20 minutes covered. Serve with cole slaw.

Jett Williams, Country Music Artist

Chicken Baked Casserole

6 large boneless, skinless chicken breast
1 small container sour cream
1 can cream of chicken soup
½ cup melted margarine
Ritz crackers

Boil chicken until tender. Chop into cubes. Add sour cream and soup, mix well. Place in lightly greased pyrex casserole dish. Crush crackers and spread over top of chicken mixture. Drizzle melted margarine on top. Bake at 350° until brown and bubbly. Enjoy!

Rick Honeycutt
Professional Baseball Player

Rick Honeycutt

Former major league and All-Star pitcher Rick Honeycutt of Catoosa County appeared in three World Series. In his 21-year professional career, he played with six teams, retiring from the St. Louis Cardinals in 1997. He was nominated for the Baseball Hall of Fame in 2002. He is currently the pitching coach for the Los Angeles Dodgers. Each year he hosts the Rick Honeycutt Golf Tournament as a benefit for young people in the county.

Chicken and Biscuits

2 ½ cups cooked premium white chunk chicken
1 can (10 ¾ oz) condensed cream of chicken soup
¾ cup milk
8 oz sour cream
1 ½ cups shredded cheddar cheese, divided
1 can of biscuits (8 count)
1 pkg (16 oz) frozen mixed vegetables
8 bacon strips, cooked and crumbled, optional

In a large bowl, combine the vegetables, chicken, soup, sour cream, milk, 1 cup cheese and bacon. Pour into an ungreased 13 x 9 inch baking dish. Cover and bake at 400° for 15 minutes.

Goolsby

Lacey Goolsby

Position: Learning Center Computer Instructor and Childcare Provider

Why literacy is important to me: Seeing people succeed is rewarding.
Favorite movie: *Iron Man*
Favorite book: Redeeming Love by Francine Rivers
Favorite quote: I believe in the sun even if it□s not shining. I believe in love even when I am alone. I believe in God even when He is silent. □ *Unknown*

Remove mixture from oven. Open biscuits and place on top of chicken mixture. Top with remaining cheese and bake uncovered for 20-22 minutes or until biscuits are golden brown.
Yields: 6 servings

Lacey Goolsby, Computer Instructor & Childcare Provider

Chicken and Dumplings

4 chicken thighs
3 cups broth from chicken
1 large pkg (about 10) refrigerated biscuits
2/3 to 1 cup milk (whole or skim)

Cook chicken thighs until very tender. There should be about 3 cups of broth remaining from chicken. Remove chicken and skin from bone. Take out excess fat according to amount desired. Let broth strike a good boil. Take one package of biscuits and add them one at a time by pinching off very small pieces until all biscuits are added. Cook about 8-10 minutes. After cooking dumplings, add 2/3 to 1 cup milk. Let this strike a good simmer to scald milk. Add chicken to dumplings if desired.

Joanne Ritchie

Chicken Pot Pie

1 lb boneless, skinless chicken breasts, cut into 1 inch pieces
¼ cup Italian dressing
4 oz Neufchatel cheese, cubed
2 tbsp flour
½ cup fat free, reduced-sodium chicken broth
1 – 10 oz pkg frozen mixed vegetables, thawed
1 refrigerated pie crust

Heat oven to 375°. Cook chicken in dressing in large skillet on medium high heat 2 minutes. Add cheese; cook and stir until melted. Add flour; mix well. Add broth and vegetables; simmer 5 minutes.

Pour mixture into deep dish 10 inch pie plate. Arrange pie crust over filling; flute edges. Cut 4 slits in crust to allow steam to escape. Bake 30 minutes or until crust is golden brown.

Nancy Peters

Chicken Pot Pie

2 to 3 lb. Hen
½ stick butter
1 chopped onion
1 cup chopped celery
1 can English peas
1 can carrots
1 cup chicken broth
1 tbsp flour
Biscuit mix for 10 biscuits

From left Dr. Ray Brooks, former president of Northwestern Technical College; T.L. Hightower, adult literacy director for Northwest Georgia; and Georgia Governor Zell Miller, present B.J. Darnell and Shirley Smith of the Learning Center the Governor's Award for workplace GED programs.

Boil hen until tender. Remove meat from bones and cut in small bite size pieces. Melt butter in ovenware pan. Add onion and celery; cook very slowly for 15 minutes. Add can of peas and carrots. Blend broth and flour. Add broth mixture, chicken, salt and pepper to taste. Top with biscuits and bake at 425° until brown. If desired, add ½ cup chopped bell pepper or can of mushrooms as onion and celery cooks.

Former United States Senator Zell Miller

U.S. Senator Zell Miller

A former history teacher, former U.S. Senator Miller worked while serving as Georgia's governor to give all Georgians a chance for a higher education. His legacy, the lottery-funded HOPE scholarship, has sent more than 500,000 Georgians to college. Also an avid fan of music, Miller authored a history of Georgia music entitled *They Heard Georgia Singing*.

Chicken Pot Pie

½ pkg frozen peas
½ cup sliced carrots
1/3 cup chopped onions
1/3 cup butter
1/3 cup flour
Salt and pepper to taste
1 ¾ cup chicken broth
2/3 cup milk
2 ½ to 3 cups cooked chicken
Store bought 2 layer pie crusts

Preheat oven to 425°. Melt butter in saucepan, stir in and cook flour for about a minute. Stir in salt, pepper, onion and carrots. Stir constantly till bubbly. Remove from heat and stir in milk and broth. Return to heat and bring to boil. Boil and stir 1 minute. Line pie plate with 1 pie crust. Pour in filling. Cover with 2nd pie crust. Crimp edges to seal. With knife, make cuts/slits in top of crust to release steam during cooking. Bake about 35 minutes.

Vanessa Channell, Ringgold Primary School

Chicken Tetrazzini

4 boneless chicken breasts
1 can cream of chicken soup
1 (8oz) sour cream
½ cup shredded Parmesan cheese
½ cup shredded cheddar cheese
1 can chicken broth
12 oz spaghetti noodles

Cook chicken breast and shred. Cook spaghetti according to package directions, drain. Mix soup, sour cream and broth together. Add chicken, stir. Add spaghetti and stir. Place in a 13x9 casserole dish. Top with cheese. Bake at 350° for 30-40 minutes. *David Austin, Computer Instructor*

Crunch-Top Chicken and Swiss Cheese Casserole

3-4 chicken breasts
6 oz Swiss cheese
2 cups herb stuffing mix
1 can cream of chicken soup
1 stick melted butter

Boil chicken, debone and cut into strips (or dice them). Place chicken in bottom of casserole dish, top with a layer of cheese and spread soup evenly over all.   In a mixing bowl, combine butter and stuffing; sprinkle on top of chicken mixture. Bake at 350° for 30-45 minutes.

Vanessa Channell, Ringgold Primary School

Easy Cheesy Chicken

2 cans chopped white chicken, drained
2 cans cream of chicken soup
1 (8oz) sour cream
2 cups cheddar cheese, shredded
1 sleeve Ritz crackers, crushed

Mix chicken, soup and sour cream. Put in a baking dish. Top with cheese, then crushed crackers. Dot crackers with butter. Bake at 350° for 20-25 minutes. Easy and good!

Dusty Nichols Murphy

"Literacy provides the greater opportunity of expression of oneself - one's thoughts, feelings, ideas, ideals, beliefs, and convictions. Hopefully encourages clarity in communication with others."
Donna Douglas

Donna's Heapin' Helpin' of Meatballs

3 lbs ground beef
1 small can carnation milk
1 cup chopped onions
2 cups oatmeal
2 eggs beaten
1 tsp garlic powder
1 tsp chili powder
½ tsp pepper
2 tsp salt

Mix together and form into meatballs.

Sauce:
2 cups ketchup
1 ½ cup brown sugar
1 tbsp liquid smoke
½ tsp salt
½ onion chopped

Mix together and pour over meatballs. Bake for one hour in a 350° oven.

Donna Douglas, Actress

Donna Douglas

As "Elly Mae" on *The Beverly Hillbillies*, Donna Douglas received all types of "schoolin" from how to cook vittles by "Granny" to how to be a sophisticated lady from "Miss Jane." In spite of "Jed's" best efforts, she never missed out on a good scrap with "Jethro." However, it was her kindness to critters of all kinds that gave the world a unique look at the sweetness of the character and made this actress an internationally known star. The former Miss New Orleans appeared on many classic television shows such as *The Twilight Zone*, *Mister Ed* and *Adam-12* and in films like *Li'l Abner*, *Lover Come Back* and *Career*. Douglas continues to appear for audiences around the world at concerts, fairs and churches, and she has recorded three well-received gospel music albums.

Doreen's Chicken Bites

4 boneless chicken breast
Oscar Meyer bacon
1/2 box brown sugar

Cut chicken breast into cubes. Cut bacon in ½ pieces. Wrap the bacon around chicken cube. Secure with toothpick. Place in baking dish. Cover completely with brown sugar. For this recipe you can ad more sugar as you like. The brown sugar baking with the meats is awesome. In the next few weeks we will give you a new twist on the chicken bites. These are a hit every where we take them and the absolute best for a wedding reception. Make 500 and watch them disappear!!!!

2007 Variation:
Mix
1 jar Orange Marmalade and 3 cups of Cattleman's BBQ sauce.
20 minutes into baking "bites" remove from oven and cover with BBQ Glaze Return to oven and continue baking until done.
This portion of "glaze" should do a 9 x 13 pan of "bites" This is a GREAT way to ad a new twist to an all time favorite.

Cherie Martin
Heart of the Home Cooking Show
on ETC

Cherie Martin

Cherie Martin is the host of *Heart of the Home* which offers recipes, tips and quick and easy ways to help you entertain guests or feed your family and make it fun. The show airs in Athens, Atlanta, Calhoun, Gilmer, Pickens, Cherokee, and Fannin counties, Copper Basin in Tennessee and Greenville, S.C. She also hosts *North Georgia Now Today* on ECTV3 in Ellijay, Ga. Visit www.heartofthe homeatetc.com

Easy Chicken Pot Pie

3 cans fat free cream of chicken soup
2 cans veg-all
1 cup chicken broth
2 cups diced chicken
½ cup chopped onion
1 cup self-rising flour
1 cup milk
1 cup mayonnaise
3 boiled eggs, diced
Black pepper to taste

Spray 9 ½ X13 inch pan with Pam. Layer onions, chicken and eggs in the bottom. Mix soup, broth, pepper and Veg-all in a sauce pan and heat. Pour over mixture in the pan. Combine mayonnaise, milk and flour in a quart jar. Cover and shake until well blended. Pour over the mixture in the pan and bake at 375° for approximately 1 hour until golden brown.

Donna Blevins, Head Start

The important thing is not to stop questioning.
Albert Einstein

Great Meat Loaf

1 ½ - 2 lbs hamburger meat (or ground turkey)
1 can tomato sauce (reserve ½ can)
1 pkg McCormick meat loaf seasoning
1 egg
bread crumbs

Mix all ingredients together. Bake 1-1 ½ hours at 350° or until done. NOTE: Reserve ½ can tomato sauce to pour on top of meat loaf before baking.

Faith Hill
Country Music Artist

Faith Hill

Five-time Grammy winner Faith Hill, who hardly has time to *Breathe* (1999), dedicates some of her energies to improving literacy rates around the country. She shouldn't need to *Cry* (2002) considering she has sold over 30 million records and has had thirteen No. 1 singles and 20 No. 1 videos and over 20 music industry awards. Her latest releases include *The Hits* (2007) and *Joy to the World*. Visit www.faithhill.com.

(Photo:Rocco Laspata: © 1999 Warner Brothers Records.)

*Reading ignites our imagination.
It teaches us to dream.*
Faith Hill

Homemade Dressing

1 loaf bread
(at least 22
slices)
2 medium
onions finely
chopped
1 ½ cups
chopped cel-
ery
1 stick butter
2 tsp salt
2 tsp sage
1 tsp poultry seasoning
2 cups salted turkey
broth (or chicken bouil-
lon)

Preheat oven to 350°.
Sauté celery and onions in
butter while tearing bread
into small pieces in a
large bowl. Add broth to
sauté. Add the seasonings
to the bread pieces and
mix. Mix all lightly
together. Turn into a
greased pan with a fork.
Bake covered with foil for
45 minutes. Remove foil
and bake an additional 10-
15 minutes. It's ready to
eat.

*Jeff Weaver
of The Rarely Herd,
Bluegrass Music Artists*

Rarely Herd

Rarely Herd, featuring Jim
Stack, Jeff Hardin, Todd Sams
and Jeff Weaver, performs
before more than one million
fans annually and provides a
never-ending collection of
comedy skits, captivating
vocals and top-notch music.
Recipients of over 120 national
and regional awards or nominations, the group is known
around the world for its unique
ability to entertain. In 2003, the
group received the Society for
the Preservation of Bluegrass
Music in America's (SPBGMA)
Grand Masters Gold award.
That honor marked for Rarely
Herd a 10-year run of being
voted by fans as Entertaining
Band of the Year.
Visit www.therarelyherd.com.

"As a songwriter and musician, learning to read and write was most necessary. Other artists that record our original songs rely on the provided tablature, score sheets and written words to help them learn the songs. As important, though I'm far from a speed-reader, I love to relax to a good book while traveling on the tour bus or plane. For me, reading and writing are a big part of quality daily life." Jeff Weaver

Hamburger Macaroni Skillet

1 lb lean ground beef
2 buttons garlic, crushed
1 large onion, sliced
12 oz. pkg macaroni
1 can kidney beans
1 can green peas
Salt to taste

Cook the macaroni until tender. Drain and set aside. In a large skillet, brown the hamburger meat with the garlic. Drain any excess grease. Add onions and continue to cook until the onions are transparent. Drain the kidney beans and green peas, add to mixture and cook about ten minutes. Add cooked macaroni and heat through. You can add Velveeta, grated Parmesan, cheddar, or any cheese you prefer to this dish.

Donna Pierce, GED Instructor

Honey Mustard Salmon

½ cup mayonnaise
2 tbsp mustard
2 green onions, chopped
1 tbsp honey
1 tsp apple cider vinegar
1/8 tsp ground black pepper
Pinch of salt
4 salmon fillets/steaks

Combine all ingredients except salmon. Reserve ½ cup of mayo ingredients, use rest to brush on salmon. Bake 375° for 15-20 minutes or until salmon is flaky.

Vanessa Channell, Ringgold Primary School

Restaurant owners Jack (left) and Karen Goodlet and Mandolinist Bill Lowery at the 2009 unveiling of the North Georgia Musicians Wall of Fame at Park Place Restaurant in Fort Oglethorpe, Ga.
(Contributed photo)

Hot Ham Sandwiches

1 stick margarine, softened
¼ cup chopped onions
¼ cup mustard
1 tbsp poppy seed
1 ½ lbs wafer thin ham
1 lb Swiss cheese, sliced
thinly
10 - 12 Buns

Combine first four ingredients. Spread mixture on both insides of buns. Place desired amount of ham and cheese on bun. Brush tops of buns with melted butter. Wrap in foil. Bake at 350° for 15 minutes or freeze for later use.

Krista Smith

CCL Task Force member

Position: Owner, Twenty Fifth Hour - Spa & Gifts

Reason for serving on the Task Force: To help others and give back to my community.

Organizations and Memberships: Member of Community Theater Group, Catoosa County Chamber of Commerce and Catoosa Citizens for Literacy

Favorite movie: Making Faces

Favorite book: Catch 22

Favorite TV show: ER

Favorite quote: Cool Beans, Groovy Pickles

Philosophy: Chill or be

Krista Smith
Catoosa Citizens for Literacy Taskforce Member

Nothing can stop the man with the right mental attitude from achieving his goal; nothing on earth can help the man with the wrong mental attitude.
Thomas Jefferson

James Earl Jones Chilean Sea Bass

10 maui onions
1 stick unsalted butter
12 roma tomatoes, seeded and chopped (or the canned, drained or canned equivalent)
5 chopped shallots
3 minced clove garlic
3 chopped basil leaves
1 tbsp extra virgin olive oil
½ cup chicken broth (if necessary)
12 pieces Chilean sea bass, 2 inches wide, 2 ½ inches long

Slice and cook onions in a skillet on low heat until caramelized (between 1 and 2 hours). Puree all ingredients except last three ingredients. Heat olive oil. Add ingredients and cook on low for 30 minutes. Add chicken broth as necessary. Season bass with salt and white pepper, to taste. Cover bass with onions and bake at 425° 10 to 12 minutes. Each of six servings should include one piece of bass over about 1/6 of the sauce.

James Earl Jones, Actor

James Earl Jones

As William in the 2005 film *The Reading Room*, James Earl Jones changed a neighborhood by changing the lives of its youth and residents one at a time. For 45 years, Jones tremendous acting talents on stage and screen and his marvelous voice have endeared him to fans around the world. He won two Tony Awards and was nominated for an Oscar for his performance as "Jack Jefferson" in the 1970 film The Great White Hope. He was the voice of the villain "Darth Vader" in *Star Wars* and the "Mufasa" in both *Lion King* films.

James Rogers' Chicken Marsala

½ stick of butter (4 tbsp)
2 tbsp olive oil
6 boneless, skinless, chicken breasts
¼ cup flour
1 large container fresh mushrooms, cleaned, drained, and sliced
1 cup Marsala cooking wine
½ cup beef broth
¼ tsp salt
fresh chopped parsley

Heat 2 tbsp butter and 2 tbsp olive oil in large skillet. Using ¼ cup flour, coat chicken breast and sauté in oil about 10 minutes on each side. Remove chicken and add mushrooms, sautéing till light brown. Add Marsala cooking wine, beef broth, and salt, simmering about 5 minutes, while scraping bottom of skillet. Add chicken back to skillet and bring to a boil, reduce and simmer 20–30 minutes basting occasionally. Remove chicken when done and place in attractive serving dish. Stir in remaining butter. Remove from heat and add fresh parsley. Stir to blend, pour over chicken and serve.

James & Debbie Rogers
Music Artist

James Rogers

Multi-genre entertainer, singer and writer James Rogers has recorded 20 albums and written over 200 songs. Rogers, who grew up in Fort Oglethorpe, Ga., entertains for most of the year at Dollywood in Pigeon Forge, Tenn. From 1994-1998 James Rogers and company won several awards including the Peoples' Choice Award for Best Show, Best Theater, and Best Entertainer. His latest CD is *Medleys and Melodies*. Visit www.jamesrogersonline.com.

Koosa (Stuffed Squash)

24 yellow squash
1 cup raw rice (I always use Uncle Ben's)
3 lbs of raw coarsely ground lean beef or lamb
Salt and pepper to taste
¼ tsp cinnamon
2 cans (8oz each) tomato sauce
1 large can of tomatoes (drained)
2-3 cloves garlic

Wash squash thoroughly. Cut off necks and reserve. Core squash, using an apple corer or the handle of an iced tea spoon to remove pulp. Combine rice, meat, salt, pepper and cinnamon and drained tomatoes. Mix well with fingers. Use this mixture to fill squash cylinders. Fill only ¾ of capacity to allow for expansion of stuffing. Pack filled squash neatly in layers in a deep, heavy pot. Pour tomato sauce around squash and liquid from tomatoes. Add enough water to cover squash. Bury garlic between squash in liquid. Bring to boil. Reduce heat and simmer, covered until squash is tender and rice is cooked about 45 minutes to an hour. Take squash necks and the inside of the squash and save for a squash casserole at a later time.
This is a wonderful meal for children...it gives them vegetables...meat and rice.

Vince and Barbara Dooley

Chickamauga-Chattanooga National Military Park

Chickamauga-Chattanooga National Military Park brings over 800,000 visitors per year to Catoosa County to visit the site of the September 1863 battle. The visitors' center provides a great introduction to the 5,300-acre park, which is marked with more than 1,400 stone monuments, cast iron tablets and bronze plaques. The park area has practically stood still in time since its dedication in 1895. (Photo by Randall Franks)

Chickamauga Battlefield
(Photo by Randall Franks)

Lemon Chili Chicken

1/3 cup lemon juice
2 tbsp olive oil
1 tbsp chili powder
3 cloves garlic, minced
2 tbsp mustard
½ tsp salt
1/8 tsp white pepper
4 whole or boneless, skinless chicken breasts

Combine all ingredients except chicken in heavy-duty zip-lock food storage bag. Add chicken; close bag and zip to close. Place in bowl or baking dish and refrigerate for 2-6 hours. When ready to cook, prepare and preheat grill. Bake at 400° or grill chicken for 12-17 minutes, turning once and brushing frequently with marinade, until chicken is thoroughly cooked. Note: I add jalapenos to make it spicy. Remove seeds and puree and add to marinade.

Phillip Whiteside, ESL Instructor

"At the desk where I sit, I have learned one great truth. The answer for all our national problems - the answer for all the problems of the world - come to a single word. That word is "education."

Lyndon B. Johnson

The Perrys

"Literacy is very important to me. I was in the ninth grade before my teachers discovered I could not read very well at all. If it was very simple reading, I could read it ok, but if it was hard reading, I was lost. After taking an evaluation test for reading, I was on a fourth grade level in reading. I was then placed in a reading class for a year. There I learned to read better than before. I was completely satisfied with what I had learned, because I felt I needed more. While selecting my subjects as a senior, I chose reading again. I was taunted by my classmates for taking this class, but I finally knew the importance of reading. Reading is used in every area of our lives. It's a very important thing to know how to do."

Libbi Perry Stuffle

For more than 30 years, the Southern Gospel music ministry of The Perrys has been touching hearts and changing lives around the U.S. As the only original member still with the group, Libbi Stuffle now travels the highways with husband Tracy, son Jared, Joseph Habedank, Troy Peach and Bryan Elliott, to reach over 200 dates per year. *Almost Morning* is the latest CD from Daywind Records. With over 30 Singing News Awards nominations, a long list of chart songs, and the 1985 Southern Gospel Music Association Horizon Award, The Perrys are helping people around the world say "Praise God, It's Settled, I'm Saved" (No. 1 song). Visit www.perryministries.com

Lib's Special Occasion Ham

10 lb spiral sliced ham
8 oz bottle of pure honey
Small can crushed pineapple
4 tbsp ground cinnamon
3 cups brown sugar
1 turkey size roaster bag

Preheat oven to 400°. Place roaster bag in side of a deep dish baking dish. Place ham inside bag. Spread sliced layers apart. In a medium size bowl, mix all the above ingredients. Mix until smooth. The mixture will be very thick. Pour mixture over ham inside the bag. After pouring the mixture over the ham, push sliced layers back together. Close the bag with the tie provided in box. With a fork or knife, punch 4 small holes in top of bag. Place the ham in the oven for 1 hour.

After one hour, remove ham from oven. Open bag on top and spoon cooked mixture over ham and sliced layers. Close bag and return to oven for another hour. When ham is done, remove ham from bone by carving. Place carved slices in another deep baking dish. After all meat has been removed from bone, take cooked mixture and pour over top of carved meat in dish. You can pour a lot or just enough to cover most of the meat.

Libbi Perry Stuffle of The Perry's
Southern Gospel Music Performers

"Lulu's Mom's Cornbread Dressing"

**2 boxes Jiffy Corn Bread Mix –
Baked ahead of time
3 cans of "Stovetop Dressing" –
2 cornbread, 1 chicken flavor
9 eggs – 6 boiled and 3 to add to
dressing
3 cans chicken broth
1 medium onion, diced
1 bunch of celery, diced
1 tbsp Morton's Nature seasoning salt
Sage, to taste, more makes it hotter
Salt and Pepper, to taste**

Crumble cornbread, add all 3 cans of Stovetop Stuffing, mix all together, add seasonings, onions, celery, diced eggs and raw eggs then chicken broth, mix well with your hands, ha! Pour into greased pan, pat with hands and bake at 350° for one hour. Enjoy!!!!

Lulu Roman, Gospel Music Artist

Lulu Roman

Comedienne Lulu Roman entertained millions every week on *Hee-Haw* from 1968-1995. She even served up quite a few plates of grub at the "Kornfield County Diner." In 2002, she became a Dove Award nominee for *Inspired*, her gospel CD. She was inducted in the Christian Music Hall of Fame in 2008. As a child she grew up in an orphanage without the commitment of a loving mother or father. She works to make life a little brighter for orphaned children. Her latest CD is *Orphan Girl*. Visit www.luluroman.net.

"Learning is knowing you can be secure in your ability to survive. This is so important, as reading is a must!!! Knowledge is power, power is security, security is an "absolute" to helping others grow in love and care. God's Care! Reading God's word is Life!!!"
Lulu Roman

Lyle Lovett's Breakfast Burrito

1 burrito size flour tortilla
1 large egg, scrambled
½ cup black beans
2 tbsp shredded cheese
Salsa

Scramble egg in egg pan. Warm tortilla in microwave and black beans in stovetop pan. Fill tortilla with scrambled egg, layer black beans on top of egg. Sprinkle shredded cheese over warm bean/egg mixture. Pour salsa, to taste, on top of mixture. Fold tortilla.

Optional: Add cilantro, sour cream, or meat to compliment your burrito.

Tommy Housworth
Actor

Caged Bird

A free bird leaps
on the back of the wind
and floats downstream
till the current ends
and dips his wing
in the orange sun rays
and dares to claim the sky

But a bird that stalks
down his narrow cage
can seldom see through
his bars of rage
his wings are clipped and
his feet are tied
so he opens his throat to sing

The caged bird sings
with a fearful trill
of things unknown
but longed for still
and his tune is heard
on the distant hill
for the caged bird
sings of freedom.

The free bird thinks of another breeze
and the trade winds soft through the sighing trees
and the fat worms waiting on a dawn-bright lawn
and he names the sky his own.

But a caged bird stands on the grave of dreams
his shadow shouts on a nightmare scream
his wings are clipped and his feet are tied
so he opens his throat to sing.

The caged bird sings
with a fearful trill
of things unknown
but longed for still
and his tune is heard
on the distant hill
for the caged bird
sings of freedom.

Maya Angelou's Jollof Rice

3 cups uncooked long grain rice
2 tbsp peanut oil
1 tsp salt
1 can (10.5 oz) beef consommé
3 cups water (about)
¼ cup peanut oil
1 ½ cups chopped onion
3 cups diced cooked ham
1 can (1lb 12oz) whole tomatoes, diced and undrained
½ can (6oz) tomato paste
2 hot dried red peppers, soaked in water, then squeezed
3 hard-cooked eggs, halved
¼ cup chopped parsley

Wash rice in warm water, changing water until it is clear.
Drain well. In a 4-quart saucepan, heat 2 tbsp oil and salt.
Add ¾ cup rice. Brown lightly, about 5 minutes, stirring frequently. Add remaining rice, consommé, and water to cover
rice about 1 inch. Lower the heat and simmer gently for 1
hour.
In 10-inch skillet, heat ¼ cup oil. Add onion and sauté until
transparent. Stir in ham, tomatoes and juice, and tomato paste.
Cover and cook over medium heat 10 minutes. Drain off 1 cup
liquid and reserve.
Add ham-tomato mixture and juice from peppers to rice,
blending well. Cover and cook until tomato mixture is
absorbed, about 3 minutes. (If rice is too dry, add a bit of
reserved liquid)
To assemble – Butter a 6-8 cup round mixing bowl. Arrange
hard cooked eggs cut side down in bottom of bowl. Sprinkle
with chopped parsley. Add rice mixture, packing firmly. Wait a
few minutes to unmold. Turn out onto serving plate.

Maya Angelou
Poet

Mazetti

2 lbs ground beef
1 lb sausage
3-4 med onions, chopped
1 large green pepper, chopped
1 stalk celery, chopped
2 small cans or 1 large can of cream of mushroom soup
1 large can tomato sauce
2 cans tomato soup
1 large jar stuffed green olives, sliced
Large bag egg noodles (cooked/drained per package directions.)

Brown ground beef and sausage, drain, add onions, pepper, and celery. Cook until tender.

In a large pan, heat soups and tomato sauce to boiling. Add meat mixture and noodles. Add olives and stir thoroughly. Pour into casserole dish and serve. (Can be refrigerated and heated later.) For extra flavor sprinkle grated cheese on top and heat in oven until cheese begins to melt.(Recipe can be cut in half or divided and frozen.)

Lynn Latimer
Catoosa Citizens for Literacy Taskforce Member

Latimer

Lynn E. Latimer CCL Task Force member

Position: Treasurer of the Catoosa Citizens for Literacy

Reason for serving on the Task Force: "It affords me the opportunity to encourage those who have not realized that education is the key that unlocks the door to success and offers a new path for those who do come to that realization."

Organizations and memberships: Mt. Vernon United Methodist Church

Favorite movie: *Pretty Woman*

Favorite book: *The Seven Last Years* by Carol Balizet

Favorite TV show: *La Femme Nikita*

Favorite quote: "This too shall pass."

Philosophy: Turn everything over to God—and leave it there.

Rebecca Holden

While portraying computer expert April Curtis on the NBC television series *Knight Rider*, Rebecca Holden invented new abilities for KITT (a talking computerized car) and new ways for KITT and Michael Knight to fight for truth, justice and the American way. She also is known for her role as the diabolical Elena on ABC's *General Hospital* and for numerous guest-starring roles on *Magnum P.I.*, *Taxi*, *Night Court*, *Mike Hammer*, *Remington Steele*, *Matt Houston* and many others. Touring internationally as a singer, the Texan not only dazzles audiences with her country and gospel music but also gives her time to charity efforts around the globe. Holden's latest inspirational album is *Dare to Dream*. Visit www.rebeccaholden.com.

Rebecca's Enchilada Casserole

1 ½ lbs hamburger meat
1 lb Velveeta cheese, grated
20 flour tortillas
1 can Trappey's Pinto Beans
1 can cream of mushroom soup
1 can cream of chicken soup
1 onion
1 small can of chopped green chilies
½ cup milk (if needed)

Brown hamburger meat and onion. Add to meat mixture: can of pinto beans (drained,optional), can of cream of mushroom soup, and can of cream of chicken soup, green chilies and milk if mixture is too thick.
Layer the following in a pan (making two layers total): 10 flour tortillas torn in pieces, meat mixture and top with grated cheese.
Layer a second time and end with grated cheese on top. Bake at 350° for 45 minutes.
Rebecca Holden Actress/Music Artist

Mexican Chicken Casserole
Serves: 5

**Chicken Tenders, boiled until done and cut in cubes
(15 ounces cooked)
2 cans reduced-fat cream of chicken soup
1 can Rotel tomatoes and green chilies (do not drain),
smash up until mushy
½ tbsp chili powder
1 tsp garlic powder
2 tbsp minced dry onion
8 oz fat-free shredded cheddar cheese
1 7 ½ ounce bag reduced-fat Nacho Doritos**

Mix together the first 6 ingredients. Crush Doritos while
still in bag. In casserole dish or rectangular cake pan,
cover bottom and sides with cooking spray. Build layers.
First place half of the Doritos in the bottom of the dish or
pan. Next, spread half of the mixed ingredients on top of
the chips. Last, sprinkle half of the cheddar cheese on top
of the mixture. Repeat all three layers. Bake at 350° for
30 minutes. Divide into five equal parts and serve.
Diamond Rio

Diamond Rio

Country music artists Diamond Rio burst onto the scene
in 1991 with theit first CD. The *Grand Ole Opry* stars won
Vocal Group of the Year six times, scored nine No. 1 hits
and 15 top-five songs while selling over 10 million
records. They share hope in songs such as the No. 1 hit "I
Believe," and "Mama Don't Forget to Pray for Me."

READING, WRITING & ARITHMETIC...

The group received the Minnie Pearl Humanitarian
Award in recognition of their many charitable endeav-
ors. They are national spokespersons for Big Brothers Big
Sisters and continually support all reading programs for
all children and adults. Visit www.diamondrio.com

Mexican Chicken Casserole

6 chicken breasts
1 (8 oz) pkg grated cheddar cheese
1 (8 oz) container sour cream
2 cans cream of chicken soup
12 corn tortillas
small can green chilies

Boil chicken until done; cut into bite sized pieces. Mix together the sour cream, chilies and soup. Cut tortillas in pieces and place in a 2-quart baking dish greased with cooking spray. Layer with chicken, soup mixture and cheese, stirring slightly. Cover and bake at 350° for 30 minutes.
Vanessa Channell, Ringgold Primary School

The Ringgold Opry, held the second Saturday night of the month, except October and December, at the historic Ringgold Depot, has been a mainstay in Ringgold since 1993. The Opry offers pickers and listeners alike a place to gather and enjoy the traditional sounds of Appalachian acoustic music. Guitarist Robert Taylor and fiddler Deborah Taylor play an old time fiddle tune.
(Photo by Randall Franks)

Mexican Lasagna

1 ½ lbs ground turkey
1-1oz. pkg taco seasoning mix
1-15oz. can diced tomatoes
2-8oz cans tomato sauce
1-4oz can diced green chilies
1 small container ricotta cheese
2 eggs, beaten
10 corn tortillas
1 lb shredded Jack cheese

Cook ground turkey in large skillet over medium heat until browned and cooked through. Drain off fat (there may not be any). Add taco seasoning mix, tomatoes, tomato sauce, and chilies. Mix well and bring to boil. Reduce heat and simmer, uncovered, 10 minutes.

Combine ricotta cheese and eggs in a small bowl.

Spread half of the turkey mixture in 13x9 inch baking dish. Place 5 tortillas over the turkey mixture. Spread half the ricotta cheese mixture over the tortillas and sprinkle with half the shredded jack cheese. Repeat layers.

Bake uncovered at 350° until cheese is melted and lightly browned for 20 to 30 minutes. Let stand 10 minutes before cutting into squares for serving. Makes 6 to 8 servings.

Annette O'Toole
Actress

Annette O' Toole

As "Martha Kent" on the long-running series *Smallville*, Annette O'Toole spent a lot of her time teaching her son, a young Superman played by Tom Welling, how to deal with his super powers. In her own 2000 series *The Huntress*, she taught the bad guys a thing or two as bounty huntress Dottie Thorson. Acting since childhood, O'Toole has been a presence on television and in film for four decades. She has garnered an Emmy nomination, a Golden Globe nomination and shares an Oscar nomination with her husband Michael McKean for Best Music, Original Song "A Kiss at the End of the Rainbow" for the 2003 film *A Mighty Wind*.

Maccheroni "all'Ultima Moda 1841" alla Napoletana
(Pasta "In the Latest Style Naples 1841")
Serves: 4-6

¾ cup olive oil
1 lb of any short tubular pasta, preferably imported Italian
3 lbs imported Italian canned tomatoes, including the juice
or 4lbs very ripe summer tomatoes
Salt
Black pepper, freshly ground
½ cup Parmigiano, freshly grated

Pour the olive oil into a crockery bowl. Add the pasta and mix
very well. Let the pasta soak in the oil for about 20 minutes.
Preheat oven to 400°. Add the canned tomatoes and all the
juice to the bowl along with salt and pepper to taste. Mix very
well, then transfer to a Pyrex casserole 14 inches in diameter.
Bake for about 45 minutes, mixing two or three times. (If
tomatoes are fresh, cut them into ½ inch thick slices and alter-
nate layers of tomato and pasta with tomatoes as top and bottom layers. Do not mix even while baking). Remove the casserole from the oven and sprinkle the cheese over the pasta mixture. Mix very well and then transfer to a serving dish. Serve
immediately without adding extra cheese.

Alan Alda
Actor, Author, Director, Writer

Alan Alda

Television Hall of Fame member Alan Alda cut his way into the fabric of American experience through his role as surgeon "Hawkeye Pierce" in the TV series *M*A*S*H*. But that was just a piece of the long tapestry that he has weaved on and off stage, screen and television as a performer, writer and director. He has been nominated for an Emmy 32 times and even as lately as 2006 garnered a nomination for an Emmy for *West Wing*, Tony for *Glengarry Glen Ross*, and an Oscar for *The Aviator* in the same year. He has won six Emmys in his career. He is also a best-selling author with his book *Never Have Your Dog Stuffed, and Other Things I've Learned*.
Visit www.alanalda.com.

'Nothing Else Like It' Meat Loaf

1 lb ground beef
1 lb ground Italian sausage
1/3 cup chopped onion
1/3 cup chopped green pepper
1 (12oz) can diced tomatoes
1 whole egg
1/3 cup bread crumbs
1 tbsp Italian seasoning

Combine all ingredients in large bowl and mix well using 'clean' hands. Divide and shape into 2 loaves. Place in 9"x13" pan. Bake at 350° for 1 hour covered 15 minutes uncovered. And while you're at it, throw a couple baking potatoes in the oven at the same time! Enjoy!

Roy Clark
Country Music Artist

The actor, comedian, legendary guitarist and banjo player hosted Hee Haw for over 20 years. As an actor he appeared in movies and on shows such as The Beverly Hillbillies. The Country Music Hall of Fame ® member won a Grammy for his recording of the "Alabama Jubilee" and enjoyed numerous charts songs. The two-time Entertainer of the Year has appeared in some of the world's biggest venues and is a member of the Grand Ole Opry. Visit www.royclark.org

186

O'Neal's Famous Dogs with Secret Slaw Recipe

Hot dog buns
Nathan's beef wieners
Fresh green onions
Hot dog relish
Ketchup
Chili
Mustard
*Secret slaw

Boil wieners, open buns and spread with ketchup and mustard on both sides. Add wiener and top with relish, green onions, chili and slaw. *Grate cabbage. Add Sweet & Low and vinegar to taste.

Judy O'Neal
UCTV-3

Judy O'Neal

Northwest Georgia media personality Judy O'Neal created a unique career through helping keep the communities she cares about informed. She owns Fort Oglethorpe's UCTV which serves Catoosa and Walker counties. While she started her media career with newspapers, she soon expanded into radio and then into television. The Rossville High School graduate served as Harry Thornton's fill-in co-host on the WDEF *Morning Show* in the 1980s and with TV 53. O'Neal hosts *Night Talk* and *The Morning Show* using her station and programming to help area causes get the word out and raise thousands of dollars each year.

Judy O'Neal and her long time co-host the late Roger Fults on the set of *Night Talk* in 2005.

187

Pecan-Crusted Chicken

4 boneless, skinless chicken breasts (1-1 ¼ lbs), trimmed
½ cup pecan halves or pieces
¼ cup plain dry bread crumbs
(I use Panko breadcrumbs)
¼ cup parmesan cheese
½ tsp salt
½ tsp pepper
1 large egg white
2 tbsp water
1 tbsp canola oil, divided

Working with one piece of chicken at a time, place between sheets of plastic wrap and pound with a meat mallet or heavy skillet until flattened to an even ¼ inch thickness. Place pecans in a food processor and pulse until the pecans are finely ground. Transfer the mixture to a shallow dish. Mix in salt, pepper, breadcrumbs, and parmesan with pecans. Whisk egg white and water in a shallow dish until combined. Dip each chicken breast in the egg-white mixture, and then dredge both sides in the pecan mixture. Heat 1 ½ tsp oil in a large non-stick skillet over medium heat. Add half the chicken and cook until browned on the outside and no longer pink in the middle, 2-4 minutes per side. Transfer to a plate and cover to keep warm. Carefully wipe out the pan with a paper towel and add the remaining oil. Cook the remaining chicken, adjusting the heat as needed to prevent scorching. Serve immediately. Makes 4 servings.

Jill Van Dyke,
Catoosa County Health Department

Peta Pleaser Veggie Wrap

6 baby bella mushrooms, sliced
2 slices medium onion
2 slices medium tomato
1 handful spinach (this ain't science, folks – use as much as ya want)
Shredded cheese (pick your fave)
Your choice of condiments (Miracle Whip works for me)
Olive Oil
1 flour tortilla (Sundried tomato tortillas are quite good with this)

Heat olive oil in a wok. Add onions, cook on medium until brown. Add mushrooms. Cook until mushrooms are hot and soft.
Heat a flour tortilla for 20 seconds. Then, add your choice of condiment, spinach, diced tomato. Spoon mushroom and onion mixture into tortilla while still hot. Sprinkle shredded cheese on top of mixture to allow cheese to melt a bit. Fold tortilla and enjoy.

Tommy
Housworth
Actor

Lori Dobbs was the Catoosa Learning Center 2008 Carter Fuller Scholarship Winner. Dobbs is presented the award by Carter Fuller and CCL co-chairman Randall Franks

Patricia Neal

As one of Tennessee's best-known native actresses, Neal won a Tony Award before she was 20 years old for her role in *Another Part of the Forest*. Her career spans stage, screen and television and among her greatest roles was her Oscar winning role opposite Paul Newman in *HUD*. She received another Oscar nomination for her work in *The Subject Was Roses* with Martin Sheen. She starred in projects such as *In Harm's Way* with John Wayne, Kirk Douglas and Henry Fonda and *A Face in the Crowd* with Andy Griffith. A stroke survivor at the age of 39, Neal has dedicated much of her time to supporting the Patricia Neal Rehabilitation Center at the Fort Saunders Regional Medical Center in her hometown of Knoxville, Tenn.

Poppy Seed Chicken

1 chicken, cut up and cooked
1 can cream of chicken soup
1 cup sour cream
1 ½ cup Ritz crackers, crushed
1 stick margarine, melted
2 tbsp poppy seeds
1 can water chestnuts or 1 small jar pimento pieces

Bone and cut up chicken pieces. Mix soup and sour cream. Combine soup mixture with chicken and water chestnuts. Place in casserole dish. Mix together cracker crumbs and margarine. Cover with poppy seeds. Bake at 350° for 25-30 minutes.
Barbara Reese, Reese Enterprises

Polly's Rolled Chicken Breasts

1 – 4.5 oz can chopped beef
4 boneless chicken breasts
8 strips bacon
1 cup sour cream
1 – 10 ¾ oz can cream of mushroom soup

Line a 1-quart casserole dish with the beef. Roll the chicken breasts up with bacon, secure with tooth-picks and place on the beef. Mix together the sour cream and soup and pour over the chicken. Bake at 300° for 1 hour and 30 minutes. Hidden Valley Ranch dressing can be substituted for sour cream. Serves 4.

Polly Lewis Copsey of The Lewis Family

Photo: The Lewis Family appears at Conasauga Bluegrass near Varnell, Ga. in 2008.
(Photo by Randall Franks)

The Lewis Family

"Pop" Roy Lewis, Miggie, Polly, Janis, "Little Roy" Lewis, Wallace, Talmadge, Esley, "Mom" Pauline and later Travis Lewis and Lewis Phillips of Lincolnton, Georgia, are called the First Family of Bluegrass Gospel. Since their beginnings in the early 1950s in Lincolnton, The Lewis Family carved a niche and musical sound that is all its own. The group was a consistent force in both the Bluegrass and Southern Gospel fields. "Pop" was inducted into the Southern Gospel Music Hall of Fame and "Mom" received the Southern Gospel Music Association's "Miss Ina" Award. In 1992, the group was inducted into the Georgia Music Hall of Fame, the into both the Gospel and Bluegrass Music Halls of Fame. Beginning in 1954 from WJBF-TV in Augusta, the television pioneers also performed a weekly show that ran every Sunday for a national record of 38 years. The group retired in the fall in 2009.
The Lewis Family won two 2009 Dove Awards for Bluegrass Album - We Are Family with Jeff & Sheri Easter and The Easter Brothers
Visit www.thelewisfamilymusic.com.

Poppy Seed Chicken

5-6 chicken breast, cooked and diced
1 can cream of chicken soup
1 cup sour cream
2 tbsp lemon juice
1 stack Ritz crackers, crushed
1 stick butter, melted poppy seeds

Ringgold's Creekwalk on Lafayette Street is a favorite place for neighbors to gather for a pleasant walk or to dangle their feet in Chickamauga Creek. (Photo by Randall Franks)

Put diced chicken in greased casserole. Mix together soup, sour cream and lemon juice. Pour over chicken. Sprinkle cracker crumbs over chicken, then drizzle butter over crackers. Blacken top of casserole with poppy seeds. Bake at 350° for 35-45 minutes.

Vanessa Channell, Ringgold Primary School

Pressure Cooker BBQ Chicken

Serves: 4

1 whole chicken, sectioned
1 cup barbecue sauce

Clean and skin chicken. Place a steamer tray in the bottom of a pressure cooker. Fill with about ½ inch of water. Toss the chicken in the barbecue sauce and place it in the pressure cooker, pouring the remaining barbecue sauce over the top of the chicken. Seal cooker. Cooking the chicken for 50 minutes, use high heat until the cooker starts to steam, then turn it down to low. The chicken will continue to cook for an additional ten minutes after it has been removed from the heat. Serve promptly. The meat will be falling off the bones.

Barbara Mandrell, Country Music Star

Fort Oglethorpe's Barnhardt Circle

Fort Oglethorpe's original bandstand sits at one end of the polo field at Barnhardt Circle in the Fort Oglethorpe Historic District. The site of the U.S. Army's Fort Oglethorpe post from 1902-1946, Barnhardt Circle was placed on the National Register of Historic Places in 1978. Fort Oglethorpe was home to the 6th Cavalry from 1919 until 1942. The Third Women's Army Corps utilized it as a training facility from 1943 until it was sold in 1946. The City of Fort Oglethorpe was established in 1949.

Gen. Patrick Cleburne

A statue of Confederate Brig. Gen. Patrick Cleburne stands in Ringgold Gap Battlefield Historical Site 1, south of Ringgold on U.S. Hwy. 41. The Patrick Cleburne Society raised funds for a bronze statue commemorating the venerated division commander of the Confederate Army of Tennessee. When the effort was incomplete Ringgold Telephone Co. decided to contribute the balance needed in excess of $50,000 as its 2012 Centennial Gift to the people of Ringgold and Catoosa County marking its upcoming 100th Anniversary. Ringgold Telephone Co. hosted a Ringgold Gap Festival in 2009. "Following the Confederate retreat from Missionary Ridge in November 1864, Cleburne's Division was ordered to delay the Federal pursuit and make a stand at Ringgold. At stake was the survival of the Army of Tennessee," said Mauriel Phillips Joslyn, author of *A Meteor Shining Brightly*. "Outnumbered four to one, Cleburne's Division of 4,000 soundly defeated the principal elements of Joseph Hooker's Union Army corps. The gallant defense of the gap saved the Army's wagon and artillery trains, and earned Cleburne the official thanks of the Confederate Congress."
(Photo courtesy the Alabama Department of Archives and History, Montgomery, Ala.)

Quiche

4 eggs, two whole eggs, and two yolks
1 ½ cups milk, heavy cream, or half and half (I use half and half)
8 strips of bacon, fried and crumbled or ½ cup ham, chopped
1 cup grated Swiss cheese
Grated parmesan cheese
Salt

White pepper
Butter, sliced
1 unbaked deep dish pie crust

Beat eggs, milk, salt and pepper together. Place the bacon or ham in the bottom of the unbaked pie crust. Sprinkle Swiss cheese over bacon or ham. Pour egg and milk mixture over the bacon and cheese. Sprinkle the top with parmesan cheese and dot with butter slices. Bake in a 350° oven for approximately 45 minutes or until the top is golden brown. After you remove the quiche from the oven, wait about 10 minutes before you slice the quiche. *Beverly Cole*

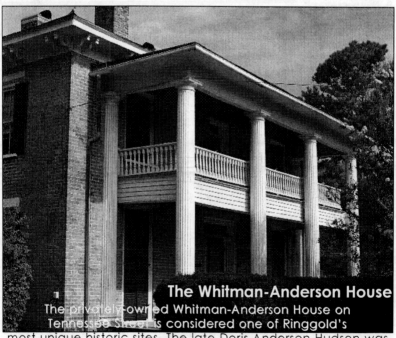

The Whitman-Anderson House

The privately-owned Whitman-Anderson House on Tennessee Street is considered one of Ringgold's most unique historic sites. The late Doris Anderson Hudson was the third generation of her family to use the residence that was built prior to the Civil War. General Ulysses S. Grant used the house as his headquarters following the Battle of Ringgold Gap.

(Photo by Randall Franks)

Rocco's Mama's Homemade Italian Red Sauce (Souga)

4 tbsp extra virgin olive oil
1 medium-large onion, processed (1/2 cup or more)
6 cloves garlic, processed (1-2 tbsp or more)
2 (28oz.) cans whole tomatoes, processed (or use crushed)
3 (12 oz) cans tomato paste
2 (28 oz) cans cold water, or more depending on desired consistency
1 tsp salt
1 tbsp pepper
2 tbsp sugar
1-2 tbsp dried sweet basil (or fresh)
2 bay leaves
Dash of cinnamon
3-4 Italian sausages (preferably Brocato's homemade)
½ lb pork shoulder (or pork ribs)
24 (2lbs) meatballs for flavor (recipe below)

Prepare meatballs using recipe below. Combine tomatoes and tomato paste. Let simmer for ten minutes to let flavors combine. Stir in water and bring to a slow boil. Add salt, pepper, sugar, and sweet basil (substitute cinnamon and bay leaves for sugar and basil for variation). Bring to slow rolling boil. Continue stirring from the bottom to prevent the sauce from sticking.

Brown pork and add to sauce along with Italian sausage. Add meatballs during last hour of cooking. Simmer for approximately 2-3 hours, stirring frequently. If any oil rises to the top, skim it off with a large spoon.

Meatballs:

2 lbs ground chuck
½ cup grated Romano cheese
¾ cup Italian seasoned bread crumbs
2-3 tbsp fresh chopped parsley
Salt, to taste
Pepper, to taste
1 medium Vidalia or yellow sweet onion, processed
3-5 small cloves of garlic
3 large eggs

Combine all ingredients and form loosely into 2" balls. Fry in skillet in vegetable oil or bake on cookie sheet in oven at 350° for 20-30 minutes. Balls will cook in sauce for at least 1 hour. The sauce (Souga) is seasoned by the simmering of all three meats in the pot.

Grace Davis, Parent Involvement Coordinator, Catoosa County Schools

Shrimp Scampi

1/3 cup oil
4 garlic cloves, minced
1 lb shrimp, peeled and deveined
1 ½ tsp Old Bay seasoning
1 tsp parsley flakes
1 tbsp. Lemon juice

Heat oil in large skillet, add garlic; sauté 1 minute or until tender. Add shrimp, seasoning, and parsley flakes; sauté 3-5 minutes or until shrimp turn pink. Stir in lemon juice. Can be served over cooked pasta or rice.
Vanessa Channell, Ringgold Primary School

Shrimp Egg Foo Yung

5 eggs
1 ½ cups coarse chopped bean sprouts
¼ lb minced shrimp
¼ cup minced water chestnuts
5 green onions (mince white bottom part, slice thin green tops)
1 tbsp soy sauce
Peanut oil to fill 1/8 inch bottom of skillet

Beat eggs, combine bean sprouts, shrimp, water chestnuts and onion bottoms. Fry, using ¼ cup portions. Remove to warm platter, cover with sauce and onion tops.

Sauce:
1 ¼ cup beef stock
2 tbsp soy sauce
¼ cup cornstarch and water mixture

Combine above and heat over medium heat until thickened.

Charley Pride
Country Music Artist

Charley Pride

Whether Charley Pride sings about "Burgers and Fries," a "Mississippi Cotton Picking Delta Town," or asks "Is Anybody Goin' To San Antone?" he conveys a way of life unique to the South and to America. He carried that music to audiences around the world and sold 70 million albums along the way. In 2000, Pride became the first African American performer inducted into the Country Music Hall of Fame. That honor was an appropriate tribute to the Country Music Association's 1971 Entertainer of the Year who had become country music's only African American superstar. In 1996, he received Turner Broadcasting's Trumpet Award marking outstanding African American Achievement. Beginning in 1969 with his first hit "All I Have to Offer You (Is Me)," he has amassed 36 No. 1 country singles. Visit www.charleypride.com

Sole Provencal

2 lbs tomatoes, seeded and roughly chopped
2 cloves garlic, finely minced
2 tbsp capers, drained
½ cup fresh basil leaves, thinly sliced
5 tbsp extra-virgin olive oil, divided
Salt
Pepper
1 ½ pounds sole filets
About ½ cup flour, for dredging

Heat oven to 400°. Combine the tomatoes, garlic, capers, basil, 2 tbsp of olive oil, ¼ tsp salt and ¼ tsp pepper in a bowl and set aside. Rinse the fish and pat dry. Lightly sprinkle with salt and pepper and dredge in flour. Heat a large skillet and add the remaining olive oil. Add several filets to the pan and cook 1 minute per side, then remove. Repeat with the remaining filets. Place the fish in one layer in a large roasting pan. Spread the tomato mixture over the top and bake until the fish flakes with a fork and is cooked through, 5 to 7 minutes. Serve over Basmati Rice Pilaf. May be served over mashed potatoes, with a side dish of a green vegetable.

Gigi Perreau, Actress

Gigi Perreau

Gigi Perreau began in Hollywood as a child actor at the age of two as Greer Garson's daughter in *Madame Curie* (1943). After appearing in over 40 films and countless TV shows, from *Gunsmoke* to the *Brady Bunch*, Perreau was one of the first to earn a star on Hollywood's Walk of Fame. She now teaches high school drama and speech and is very involved in the arts and their influence and impact on literacy. She recently participated in movies *Fly Me to the Moon*, *Around the World in 50 Years* and *Time Again*.

"As a former child star, I'm finding that my career as a Drama teacher at the high school level gives me a wonderful opportunity to give back, and encourage my students to read a great deal.
I explain that 'the more you read, the better prepared you are to create diverse characters'. They are also encouraged to read plays of all kinds from Shakespeare to modern drama."

Gigi Perreau

Susan Gregg Gilmore's autographs copies of her book "Looking for Salvation at the Dairy Queen" as part of the One Book, One Community program at the Colonnade Oct. 9, 2008.

Catoosa Citizens for Literacy continues to seek ways to break the cycle of illiteracy

By Randall Franks

Catoosa Citizens for Literacy and the Catoosa County Library coordinates a joint One Book One Community program.
"In Catoosa County, every month is literacy month," said

READING, WRITING & ARITHMETIC...

Shirley Smith, executive director. "However, we celebrate September as International Literacy Month."
In celebration of this month in 2008, CCL and the public library sponsored "Looking for Salvation at the Dairy Queen" author, Susan Gregg Gilmore coming to the community.
"All citizens of Catoosa County were encouraged to read the book," she said. "'Looking for Salvation at the Dairy Queen' is a fantastic fiction novel which takes place in Ringgold, Ga. about a little girl, Catherine Grace Cline who wants to find the fastest way out of town. As Susan Gregg Gilmore says in her novel, 'Sometimes you have to return to the place where you began, to arrive at the place where you belong.'
"This was an appropriate book to start our One Book, One Community. Susan is a talented novelist from whom we hope to see much more."
The project continued in 2009 with an outstanding evening with Georgia author Terry Kay and a focus on his book "To Dance with the White Dog."

Above: Terry Kay with Patrick Sharrock

Right: Terry Kay visits with Nancy Everett.

Stuffed Peppers in a Hurry

2 lbs lean ground beef
1 large can tomatoes
2 cups minute rice
2 cups water
3 large bell peppers, cut in 1" squares
Salt, to taste
Pepper, to taste
Brown the ground beef, add the tomatoes, rice, water, and bell peppers. Cook until peppers are tender and season to taste. For a stronger tomato flavor, I add about a tablespoon of tomato paste.
Donna Pierce, GED Instructor

6th Cavalry Museum

The 6th Cavalry Museum on Barnhardt Circle in Fort Oglethorpe, Ga.
The museum commemorates the "Fighting 6th's" involvement in conflicts ranging from the Spanish-American War to Operation Desert Storm. The museum is open Tuesday - Saturday 9 a.m.- noon and 1 p.m. - 4 p.m. Admission is $3.

Sunnyside Eggs

2 large eggs
Butter

Heat an iron pan on medium heat until handle is uncomfortably warm to hold. Butter should sizzle when applied, but not burn.

Break the egg shell gently into pan. Cover immediately. Cooking proceeds rapidly – DO NOT OVERCOOK— If whites are still liquid when cover is removed for inspection, add a few drops of water and replace cover for 45 seconds. Serve on oven-warmed plate 170°. Bon Appetite.

Allan Arbus, Actor

Allan Arbus

When many TV fans think of Allan Arbus, what quickly comes to mind is his role as psychiatrist "Maj. Sidney Freedman" in the TV series M*A*S*H, but the actor has brought characters to life on many classic TV shows and films since the 1960s often finding himself in the role of a doctor. Some of these shows are *Wonder Woman*, *Hardcastle and McCormick*, *In the Heat of the Night*, *Judging Amy*, *NYPD Blue*, and *Matlock*.

Historical Markers in Catoosa County

It's easy to drive by the historical markers on the side of the highway and not notice what they commemorate. There are many markers in the county honoring various battle sites, Civil War hospitals, pioneer settlements and churches, including:

"4th Corps' Route to Tunnel Hill," located at Old Tunnel Hill Road, 1/2 mile south of Ga. 2 east of U.S. Hwy. 41

"Atlanta Campaign, Ringgold Gap, May 7, 1864," located at United States Department of Interior pavilion on U.S. Hwy. 41 southeast of Ringgold

"Battle of Chickamauga," located at triangular park on U.S. 41 in Ringgold

"Blue Star Memorial Highway," located on I-75 at Ga. Welcome Center

"Campaign for Atlanta Began Here," located at Ga. 2 at Old Tunnel Hill Road, east of U.S. Hwy. 41

"Catoosa County Courthouse," located in downtown Ringgold

"Catoosa Springs Confederate Hospitals," located on Keith Road just north of Ga. 2 and east of U.S. Hwy. 41

"Cherokee Springs Confederate Hospital," located 1/2 mile down Cherokee Valley Road .3 mile east of U.S. 41, south of Ringgold

"Confederate Hospitals," located at Courthouse in Ringgold

"Leet's Tanyard," located at Beaumont and Mount Pisgah Roads, west of Ga. 151 southwest of Ringgold

"Nickajack Gap," located at Ga. 151 at Wood Station, eight miles south of Ringgold at the road to the gap

"Old Federal Road," located at U.S. Hwy. 41 just south of Pine Grove Baptist Church north of Ringgold

"Old Federal Road," located on Ga. 2 just east of U.S. Hwy 41 at Tiger Creek

"Old Stone Presbyterian Church War Time Hospital," located at Ga. 2 just east of U.S. Hwy. 41 at Tiger Creek

"Ringgold Gap, November 27, 1863," located at U.S. 41 at Ringgold pavilion.

"The Napier House," located at Burning Bush and Redbelt Roads

"The Whitman-Anderson House," at 309 Tennessee Street in Ringgold

"Western & Atlantic Depot," located at Depot Street and U.S. 41 in Ringgold

READING, WRITING & ARITHMETIC...

Sacred Sounds Fridays at the Ringgold Depot

A collaborative non-profit with the Catoosa Citizens for Literacy, the Share America Foundation, hosts gospel concerts on second weekends of the month 10 times a year. The program encourages youth in the traditional music of Appalachia while providing the Pearl and Floyd Franks Scholarship to eligible musicians and singers. Top: Catoosa County designee Emily Hullender receives her award with (from left) her father Jeff Hullender, president Randall Franks, and supporters Jerry and Jan-Buckner Goff on hand. Bottom: Catoosa County designee Deborah Taylor performs with Randall Franks (left) and Lewis Taylor.
Visit www.shareamericafoundation.org or www.myspace.com/shareamerica

Photos courtesy
Share America
Foundation

Tex-Mex Enchiladas

4 cups chicken, cooked and diced
2 cups Mexican cheese blend, shredded and divided
1 small red onion, chopped
1 can (15oz) enchilada sauce, divided
8 10-inch flour tortillas

Preheat oven to 400°. Coat a 9x13 baking dish with non-stick cooking spray. In a medium bowl combine the chicken, 1 cup cheese, onion and ¾ cup enchilada sauce; mix well. Divide the mixture evenly among the centers of the tortillas. Tightly roll up the tortillas and place seam side down in the baking dish. Top with remaining enchilada sauce and sprinkle with remaining cheese. Bake 15-18 minutes or until cheese is melted and the enchiladas are heated through. Serve immediately.

Delores Turner

The Brotherton Cabin at Chickamauga Battlefield (Photo by Randall Franks)

Texas Meat Marinade

½ tsp dry mustard
½ tsp thyme
½ tsp marjoram
½ tsp fresh ground pepper
1 tsp Yucatan Sunshine Habanero Pepper Sauce
1 tbsp Worcestershire sauce
2 tsp chopped garlic
¼ cup corn oil
¼ cup olive oil
½ tsp salt

Mix the dry mustard, thyme, marjoram, and pepper together. Then add garlic, Worcestershire sauce, hot pepper sauce, corn oil, and olive oil. Mix well and pour over your meat of choice covering entire piece of meat with mixture. Marinate for a few hours. Sprinkle with salt just before cooking.

Former First Lady Laura Bush

"Read, read, read. Read everything - trash, classics, good and bad, and see how they do it. Just like a carpenter who works as an apprentice and studies the master. Read! You'll absorb it. Then write. If it's good, you'll find out. If it's not, throw it out of the window."

William Faulkner

Tomato Pie

4 medium tomatoes, sliced
½ tsp basil
½ cup onion, chopped
1 cup mozzarella cheese, grated
1 cup cheddar cheese, grated
1 cup mayonnaise
1 pie crust

Preheat oven to 350°. Cook pie shell for 10 minutes, remove from oven and cool. Layer tomato slices, basil and onion in pie shell. Add salt and pepper to taste. Mix grated cheeses and mayonnaise together. Spread on top of tomatoes. Bake 30 minutes. Cool slightly before serving.

This recipe was from our great aunt. She passed away in 1982 at the age of 83. My grandchildren love this dish and beg for it all the time. Blaine Helton

Robert Hitchcox of Chattanooga Coca Cola Co. takes some spelling lessons in 2007 from young tutor Haynie Gilstrap who participates in the Catoosa Ferst Foundation for Childhood Literacy program which provides free books every month to more than 2,000 registered youth in the county, up to age five. One of its annual fundraisers is the Ferst Adult Spelling Bee. The Catoosa Citizens for Literacy helped to launch the program and continues to support its efforts.

Tim McGraw's Chicken & Dumplings

1 small hen
water
2 cups all-purpose flour
Pinch of salt
Milk
1 egg

Boil hen, adding salt to taste. When tender, pull chicken from the bone and return to the broth. Pour flour into a bowl, leaving a hole in the middle. Add 1 egg and enough milk to form a doughy consistency (similar to how you would make biscuits). Sprinkle flour on cutting board. Pinch off part of the dough and roll into a thin sheet and cut into squares. Drop one square at a time into broth. Continue this until all of the dough is used. Add salt and pepper to taste and simmer until tender.

Tim McGraw

Tim McGraw's latest CD is *Reflected: Greatest Hits V. 2.* He has sold 40 million albums and singles worldwide. His amazing career encompasses 30 No. 1 singles.
He has won three Grammy's, 11 Academy of Country Music awards, 11 Country Music Association awards, nine American Music Awards and three People's Choice awards.
McGraw has appeared in four films including *Friday Night Lights, Flicka, The Kingdom* and *Four Christmases.*
Visit www.timmc-

Tim McGraw
Country Music Artist and Actor

Tracy Byrd's Shrimp Bread Loaf

Tracy Byrd

1 lb shrimp
1 loaf French bread
1 white onion, chopped
1 cup of shredded cheddar cheese
1 stick of butter or margarine
Salt
Pepper
Tony Chasre's Cajun Seasoning or Red Pepper and Paprika

Cut shrimp into small (1/2 inch pieces, then sauté in butter and onion over medium heat for about 5 minutes. Cut French bread loaf in half, long ways. Take the top half and scrape out the center so it looks like a boat. Take the crumbs and spread them on a cookie sheet. Toast the crumbs and the hollow loaf until brown. Combine crumbs with sautéed shrimp and onions, mix thoroughly. Stuff mixture into hollowed half of the loaf and spread cheese over the top. Bake at 350° for 3-5 minutes or until cheese is melted.

Tracy Byrd, Country Music Artist

Tracy Bryd began his climb to the top of the charts in Texas. In 1993, he reached the No. 1 slot with his third single, "Holdin' Heaven." He has enjoyed success with his traditional country sounds of several chart singles, "Lifestyles of the Not So Rich and Famous," "Someone to Give My Love To" and the title single from the album *That's the Thing About A Memory. Its About Time* everyone sees that Byrd is *No Ordinary Man* (two more of Byrd's albums).

In his latest project *Different Things* he explores his latest musical expressions. Visit tracybyrd.musiccitynetworks.com.

Tracy Lawrence's Mama's Chicken Casserole

1 whole chicken
2 stalks celery
1 small-medium onion
1 can tomato soup
1 can cream of celery
1 can cream of mushroom soup
1 can cream of onion
1 can Rotel tomatoes with chilies
Garlic powder to taste
1 bag broad egg noodles
shredded cheese

Tracy Lawrence

Boil whole chicken and de-bone (keep chicken broth to boil egg noodles). In saucepan, sauté with butter chopped celery and onion. In separate pot, combine soup mixtures and cook over medium heat until well heated. Add celery and onions to soup. Boil egg noodles in chicken broth, drain and place in casserole dish. Place bite sized chicken pieces over noodles and pour soup mixture on top. Cover with shredded cheese and place in oven at 400° until cheese is melted.

Tracy Lawrence, Country Music Artist

In his 1996 double platinum CD *Time Marches On*, Tracy Lawrence beckons people back to "simpler things." After eighteen years of country hits like "Texas Tornado" and "One Step Ahead of the Storm," Lawrence continues to sing up a storm as he lights up the stage wherever he performs. His latest CD is "The Rock." Visit tracylawrence.com.

211

Turkey Meatloaf

1 ½ lbs lean ground turkey
1 onion, chopped
4 egg whites
1 cup salsa
¾ cup old-fashion oats, uncooked
1 pkg Knorr Vegetable Soup mix or Ranch Dressing Mix (dry)
¼ tsp ground black pepper
½ cup ketchup

Preheat oven to 350°. In a large mixing bowl, combine all ingredients except for ketchup. Press mixture into 9 x 5 loaf pan and spread ketchup over top. Bake until meatloaf is no longer pink in the center and juice is clear, about 1 hour.
Vanessa Channell, Ringgold Primary School

Kweisi Mfume

(GED recipient)

Kweisi Mfume is a former United States Congressman from Maryland, and former President and Chief Executive Officer of the National Association for the Advancement of Colored People (NAACP). He is also a GED recipient, he graduated magna cum laude from Morgan State University. In 1984, he earned a Masters degree in liberal arts with a concentration in International Studies from Johns Hopkins University. A former radio and television host, he is the recipient of hundreds of awards, proclamations and citations. His best-selling autobiography is entitled *No Free Ride*.

Whole Wheat Rigatoni w/ Homemade Tomato Sauce

12 cloves garlic, peeled and crushed
1 lb whole wheat rigatoni
6 fresh plum tomatoes, diced
1 cup mushrooms, sliced
1 red pepper, sliced
½ cup black olives, cut in half
½ cup parmesan, grated
4 tbsp chopped Italian parsley
2 cups vegetable stock
2 tbsp olive oil
Pinch of pepper flakes
Salt and Pepper

Bring 2 quarts of water to a boil. In a medium sauce pan, sauté the crushed garlic in half the olive oil until fragrant. Add the fresh tomatoes, crushed pepper flakes, and vegetable stock and simmer slowly for 30 minutes. Season with salt and pepper. Cook the rigatoni. Drain. In the larger pot, pour the rest of the olive oil, sauté red pepper, black olives, and mushrooms until tender. Then add the rigatoni and homemade tomato sauce, and toss all together. Finish with parsley and sprinkle with parmesan cheese. Serve warm. (Serves 6)

Former First Lady Laura Bush

Zesty Broiled Flounder

3 tbsp mayonnaise
1 tbsp fresh ginger, grated
2 tsp prepared horseradish
2 tsp light brown sugar
4 tsp soy sauce
1 small garlic clove, minced
2 (6 oz) flounder filets, or halibut
Cooking spray
Fresh parsley, chopped

Combine first 6 ingredients in a small bowl. Brush mayonnaise mixture on both sides of fillets. Place fillets on a lightly greased, shallow baking sheet, and sprinkle with breadcrumbs. Coat breadcrumbs with cooking spray. Bake at 450° for 15 minutes or until fish flakes easily with a fork. Sprinkle with parsley. Makes 2 servings.

Shirley Smith, Executive Director

The Colonnade provides an entertainment venue for Catoosa County. Community theatre productions from groups such as The Community Players bring laughter to thousands each year. Susan Clark (left) and Gayle Carter appear as "Miss Maude" and "Miss Myrtle." (Photo courtesy The Community Players)

Vegetable Chicken Casserole

1 can chopped water chestnuts
2 large skinless boneless
chicken breasts, cut into
bite-size pieces
1 stick margarine
2 small scallions
½ tsp garlic salt
1 cup sour cream
1 cup Kraft mayonnaise
1 tbsp onion bits
½ tsp. salt
½ tsp. black pepper
1 pkg saltine crackers
1 can (28 oz) VegAll
1 bag (8 oz) shredded cheddar
cheese

Sammy Ward

Mix in casserole dish VegAll, water chestnuts, cheese, sour cream, mayonnaise, onion bits, salt, black pepper and garlic salt. Set aside. In saucepan sauté bite size chicken and scallions in ½ stick margarine. Then mix with other ingredients. Bake at 300 degrees for about 23 minutes. Remove from oven and add cracker crumbs mixed with ½ stick melted margarine. If mixture is too dry add more melted margarine. Sprinkle on top of casserole. Return casserole to oven and bake until golden brown, about 6 to 7 minutes. Serves 4 to 6.
Linda Ward
Mother of Sammy Ward
Contemporary Christian Artist

Contemporary Christian artist and Ringgold, Georgia, native Sammy Ward reached the youth of America with his CD *My Passion*. Ward's unique vocal performances and songwriting on songs such as "It's For You" help to set him apart from other performers as his songs hit charts around the world. He writes songs for Universal Music Publishing Group. "It's very important for me as a believer to be on track and be a clean vessel for God's use," he said in 2003.

215

The Old Stone Church

The Old Stone Church is one of Catoosa County's oldest structures built in 1850. The Catoosa County Historical Society operates it as a museum. Originally known as Chickamauga Presbyterian Church, the building was used as a Civil War Hospital. Bloodstains from medical procedures conducted there are still visible in the wood floor. Teeth marks from the Union horses can still be found on the original pews that were used by the Yankees to feed their animals. During and following the Reconstruction period, the church was a center for community activity. The church hosted one of the first known performances of E. A. Hoffman's and A.J. Showalter's "Leaning on the Everlasting Arms." Showalter attended a morning service, took dinner at the nearby Magill Family home where he took out the words shared with him by Hoffman and he finished the melody on the family piano. He then performed it when returning to the evening service at the church. The site also hosted legendary 1800s evangelist Dwight L. Moody during a Southern tour. Singer Ira Sankey also appeared.

(Church Photo by Randall Franks)

Showalter

Orientation
(Soups & Salads)

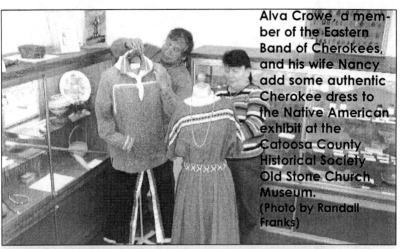

Alva Crowe, a member of the Eastern Band of Cherokees, and his wife Nancy add some authentic Cherokee dress to the Native American exhibit at the Catoosa County Historical Society Old Stone Church Museum.
(Photo by Randall Franks)

Richard Taylor

Chief Taylor

One of Catoosa County's earliest notable citizens was Richard Taylor, assistant chief of the Cherokees.

Taylor's Crossroads centered around his 150-acre plantation, Mount Hope, which stood on a hill near the Alabama Highway location of Kentucky Fried Chicken and Waffle House. Taylor operated an inn, a tavern, saw and grist mills, and a tollgate. His settlement would eventually become Ringgold.

"When compared with his times and contemporaries, he was probably the most outstanding man the Catoosa County area has produced," said William H.H. "Bill" Clark, in his book "History in Catoosa County."

As a leader of the Cherokee Nation, Chief Taylor represented the Chickamauga District of the original Cherokee Nation as a delegate to Washington, and on numerous occasions met with several presidents.

In 1816, Taylor was among a six-member delegation that met with Pres. James Madison. According to Clark's book, the delegation became the toast of Washington Society during its visit.

In 1831, Taylor led a delegation to Washington trying to plead the case of the Cherokee Nation whose rights were being stripped away by the state of Georgia.

With the decision by Pres. Martin Van Buren to force the removal of the remaining Cherokees in 1838 from their lands, the Trail of Tears occurred.

Sending his own family earlier, Taylor led a group that left for Oklahoma on Sept. 20, 1838. The group arrived in Oklahoma on March 24, 1839.

His party consisted of 51 wagons, 358 riding horses and 897 persons, with 15 births and 55 deaths reported on the journey.

Ringgold City Council honored Taylor with the Chief Richard Taylor Nature Trail in 2008 which winds along Chickamauga Creek on land that was once part of his Mount Hope.

Apple Salad

1 small can crushed pineapple, undrained
½ cup sugar (I use Splenda)
¼ cup flour
3 Granny Smith apples
1 small container Cool Whip (I use FREE)
In a microwavable container, mix crushed pineapple, sugar, and flour. Blend well, and microwave on medium power for 6 minutes. Allow to cool slightly.
In food processor, pulse unpeeled, sliced apples until coarsely chopped.(Or you can dice apples by hand…I never have the patience!)
In a large bowl, blend cooled pineapple mixture with apples, then add Cool Whip, and mix. Refrigerate till ready to serve.
(This salad lasts very well in the fridge.)
Marcia Kling, TV Journalist

Asian Chicken Salad

1 cooked whole chicken breast, diced
½ cup red pepper, diced
4 scallions, sliced
2 tbsp mayonnaise
2 tsp soy sauce
1 tsp sesame oil
Garnish with crushed black pepper, to taste.
To cook chicken, bring 1 quart of water to a boil, add chicken breast, reduce heat and simmer for 20 minutes. Mix together mayonnaise, soy sauce, and sesame oil to make dressing.
Combine remaining ingredients and add dressing. Makes 3 cups.
Vanessa Channell, Ringgold Primary School

Buttermilk Salad

1 can (20oz) crushed pineapple
2 cups buttermilk
1 (8oz) cool whip
1 box (6oz) Jell-O, any flavor
½ cup chopped nuts

Place undrained pineapple and jell-o in a saucepan. Heat until jell-o has completely dissolved. Remove from heat and cool. When it is well cooled, stir in buttermilk. Fold in cool whip. Pour into serving dish. Refrigerate until it has congealed (several hours). You will be surprised how good it is!
Karen Austin

Annette Newton's Cranberry Congealed Salad

1 large box or 2 small boxes sugar-free cranberry Jell-o
1 can cranberry sauce
1 medium can pineapple tidbits (in it's own juice)
1 small can crushed pineapple (in it's own juice)
1 tart apple, chopped
½ cup celery, diced
½ cup pecans, chopped
1 cup pineapple juice

Drain pineapple and reserve 1 cup juice (add water if not enough juice to make 1 cup). Heat juice and dissolve Jell-o in juice. Add cranberry sauce and dissolve as much as you can. Add all other ingredients. Mold or put in a serving bowl. Refrigerate until set. Serve with whipped topping if desired.
Donna Blevins, Head Start

Crazy Good Fruit and Pretzel Salad

2/3 cup sugar
8 oz pkg cream cheese, softened
24 oz cool whip
2 cans (11 oz) mandarin oranges, drained
2 cans (20 oz) pineapple tidbits, drained
1 cup sugar
1 cup melted butter
2 cups crushed pretzels

Combine 2/3 cup sugar and cream cheese. Fold in cool whip. Stir in well-drained mandarin oranges and pineapple. Mix and set in refrigerator. Mix 1 cup sugar melted butter and pretzels. Spread in lipped baking sheet. Bake at 400° for 7 minutes. Let cool and break apart. Mix half of pretzel mix into fruit salad. Transfer to 9x13 pan. Just before serving, top with remaining pretzel mixture. Can make a day ahead, but don't put topping on until ready to serve.

Jayme Elliott,
Communities In Schools

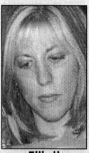

Jayme Elliott CCL Taskforce member
Position: Director, Communities In Schools
Elliott
Business: Catoosa County Schools

Reason for Serving on the taskforce: The Learning Center is all about helping people with great hearts and dreams. The Learning Center gets them the resources they need so that they are one step closer to their educational and life goals!

Organizations and Memberships: Catoosa Citizens for Literacy, Catoosa County Family Connection, Will Work 4 Kids, Ringgold Band Boosters

Favorite TV show: *House*

Favorite Quote: "Humor is the great thing, the saving thing. The minute it crops up, all our irritations and resentments slip away and a sunny spirit takes their place." Mark Twain

Egg Salad a la George

6 eggs
Mayonnaise
Whole wheat or white bread
Salt and pepper
Place eggs in room temperature water
to cover by 1 inch. Bring water to boil
and let boil about 10 minutes until
eggs are hard cooked. Run cold water
over eggs to cool. Drain, peel and
chop eggs. Place finely chopped eggs
in a bowl and mix with just enough
mayonnaise to moisten. Season with
salt and pepper. Serve as sandwich
spread on whole wheat or white bread.
Former First Lady Laura Bush

15th Wisconsin Infantry
monument at
Chickamauga
Battlefield
(Photo by Randall Franks)

English Pea Salad

1 head lettuce, chopped
1 cup celery, chopped
1 can water chestnuts, sliced
1 cup bell pepper chopped
1 cup green onions, chopped
1 lb bag frozen English peas (microwave 5 minutes)
1 cup mayonnaise
2 tbsp sugar
1 cup grated cheddar cheese
Toss together lettuce, celery, chestnuts, bell pepper and onions.
Layer in bottom of dish. Pour peas over mixture. Mix mayonnaise and sugar together and spread over peas. Sprinkle cheese
on top. Very tasty.
Wilma Hopper

222

5-String Cabbage And Chicken Salad

1 medium cabbage, chopped
1 bunch green onions, sliced
1 cup toasted slivered almonds
4 tbsp sesame seeds, toasted
2 pkgs "Top Ramen" Chicken Oriental soup
2 whole chicken breasts, precooked and cut into small pieces

Put all ingredients in large bowl. Sprinkle one flavor packet from "Top Ramen" over salad. Set aside other packet for dressing.

Dressing:

4 tbsp sugar
1 cup oil
6 tbsp (oriental) rice vinegar
1 tsp pepper
½ tsp salt
1 "Top Ramen" flavor packet

Shake and pour over salad. Toss salad. Keeps well and makes lots. There are other oriental noodle soups. Any "Ramen" type is fine.

Mike Scott
Bluegrass Music Artist

(Photo: Kim Lancaster Photography)

Mike Scott

In his latest release, *Blue Moon of Kentucky, a Tribute to Bill Monroe*, Banjo stylist Mike Scott again brings an enthusiasm and excitement to every note he plays. Performing since the age of ten, Scott has entertained audiences not only with his own show but also as part of Carl Story's Rambling Mountaineers, Jim and Jesse's Virginia Boys, Danny Davis and the Nashville Brass and Ronnie Reno and the Reno Tradition.
Visit
www.mikescottmusic.com

LOW-FAT TUNA PASTA SALAD

4 oz. bow-tie pasta
1 cup red and green grapes, halved
1 can tuna, or chicken, well drained
¼ cup lemon flavored, low-fat yogurt
½ cup walnuts, coarsely chopped

Cook pasta according to package directions. Flake the tuna and add remaining ingredients. Toss together lightly. Serve on lettuce leaves if desired.

Donna Blevins, Head Start

Eddie Murphy

Actor and comedian Eddie Murphy gained w o r l d w i d e acclaim nearly two decades ago through his work on *Saturday Night Live* and in the films *48 Hours* and *Beverly Hills Cop*. His recent film successes include the animated smash *Shrek*, *Dr. Doolittle* and *The Nutty Professor*.

Enos' Daisy White Salad

1 can of white cherries, pitted and drained
½ lb miniature marsh-mallows
1/4 lb blanched slivered almonds
juice of ½ lemon
1 egg white
1 pt of whipping cream

Beat the egg white and cream together. Gently toss in the cherries, marshmallows, almonds and lemon juice and chill for at least a few hours.

Paula & Sonny Shroyer, Actor

Sonny Shroyer

Sonny Shroyer, as "Coach Bear Bryant" in the film *Forrest Gump*, helped to encourage Forrest, played by Tom Hanks, to find his strength running down an Alabama football field. As "Enos" in the *Dukes of Hazzard*, Shroyer found his own strength in always believing the best in people. "Enos couldn't even believe that 'Boss Hogg' would do anything wrong," Shroyer said. "They had to rein-force Enos's faith in humanity." In the end, no mat-ter what get-ahead scheme "Sheriff Roscoe" and "Boss Hogg" conjured up, their winnings would wind up going to charity or to helping someone. Starring in his own CBS series *Enos*, Shroyer was nominated for two People's Choice Awards. Shroyer has appeared in numerous films including *The Longest Yard*, *Smokey and the Bandit* and *Roots*. In one of his 2009 film *The Way Home* with Dean Cain and Lori Beth Edgeman he gives an uplifting performance which changes the course of all the char-acters lives. Over the last few decades he has made guest appear-ances in several television series including *I'll Fly Away*, *In the Heat of the Night* and *The Love Boat*. Visit www.sonnyshroyer.com

Layered Salad

1 pound fresh spinach, washed and torn
1 small head red leaf lettuce, washed and torn
1 medium red onion, thinly sliced
2 ½ cups mayonnaise (low-salt)
½ teaspoon garlic powder
6 hard-cooked eggs, sliced
1 10 oz. pkg. Frozen early peas, thawed
1 6 oz. pkg salami, cut into strips
8 ounces Swiss cheese, cubed (low-salt)
1 6 oz. pkg cooked or smoked ham, cut in strips

Page

Combine spinach, lettuce and red onion. Place half of salad greens in a large (5-quart) salad bowl. Combine mayonnaise and garlic powder; mix well, and spread half of mixture evenly over salad greens. Layer in order: egg slices, peas, salami strips, cheese cubes, remaining salad greens, and ham strips. Spread remaining mayonnaise mixture over top, sealing to edge of bowl. Cover tightly and refrigerate overnight.

Pat Page CCL Task Force Member
Former Catoosa County Commissioner

The Catoosa County Citizen's and Veteran's Memorial at Benton Place Campus honors all who have served both at home and abroad. Bricks can be purchased honoring family members.

Mexican Cornbread Salad
Serves: 8

1 pkg (6oz) Mexican cornbread mix
1 can (4 ½ oz) chopped green chilies, undrained
Dash of sage
1 package (1oz) ranch style dressing mix
8 oz sour cream
8 oz mayonnaise
2 cans (15 ½ oz) whole kernel corn, drained
2 cans (16 oz) pinto beans, rinsed and drained
1 cup green pepper, chopped
3 large tomatoes, chopped
10 slices of cooked and crumbled bacon
1 pkg (8oz) shredded cheddar cheese
1 cup green onions, sliced

Farmer

Knox Farmer, CCL Co-Chairman

Position: V.P. Branch Operations and Sales
Business: Northwest Georgia Bank
Organizations & Memberships: Fort Oglethorpe Kiwanis, Hutcheson Foundation Board Member, Joint Chair for Catoosa Citizens for Literacy, BBC Board Member
Favorite Movie: Jeremiah Johnson
Favorite Book: The Difference Maker
Favorite TV Show: The Dog Whisperer
Favorite quote: " You can never cross the ocean unless you have the courage to lose sight of the shore" Christopher Columbus
Philosophy: "Our lives begin to end the day we become silent about things that matter." – Martin Luther King, Jr.

Prepare cornbread as directed on package with chilies and sage. In mixing bowl, combine dressing mix, sour cream and mayonnaise. Set aside. Crumble half of cornbread then top with half of the beans, half sour cream mixture, half green peppers, half of the remaining ingredients (in any order), then repeat. Cover and chill for at least two hours.

Knox Farmer, Co-Chairman, Catoosa Citizens for Literacy

Tabooley (Cracked Wheat Salad)

"There are many versions of this salad, but the one that I grew up with I like the best." – Barbara Dooley.

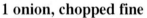

1 cup fine burghol
(cracked wheat)
5 bunches of parsley, stemmed and chopped fine
1 onion, chopped fine
½ cup fresh mint chopped fine
½ cup fresh mint chopped fine
4 lbs tomatoes chopped (these should be summer tomatoes to make this salad wonderful)
¼ to ½ head of iceberg lettuce depending how much lettuce you want in it.
½ cup fresh lemon juice
¼ cup olive oil
Salt, to taste
Pepper, to taste

Soak the burghol in water to cover. It will expand greatly. After 30 minutes, squeeze the burghol with your hands to drain it, and place it in a bowl. Chop the tomatoes on top of the wheat, that gives the wheat extra flavor. Add the remaining ingredients and mix well. You might have to add a little more lemon juice and oil depending on your tastebuds. I have a hard time giving the exact ingredients because I really cook by taste.

Vince and Barbara Dooley

ORIENTATION

Strawberry Congealed Salad

1 large pkg strawberry Jell-O
2 cup boiling water
1 (10oz) package frozen strawberries
1 small can crushed pineapple
½ cup sugar
1 tsp vanilla extract
1 envelope Dream Whip
8 oz cream cheese
Chopped nuts to sprinkle on top

Dissolve Jell-O in boiling water and reserve ¼ of the mixture. Mix the remaining Jell-O with the strawberries and pineapple. Pour into oblong dish and refrigerate until firm. Mix Dream Whip with the ¼ reserved Jell-o using a mixer at medium speed. Combine cream cheese, sugar and vanilla with the Jell-O/Dream Whip mixture and beat until smooth. Pour over the congealed mixture. Sprinkle chopped nuts on top and refrigerate. (Works well with low fat and no sugar variety products.)

Donna Blevins, Head Start

White Salad Dressing

2 eggs
1 cup sugar
¼ cup vinegar
2 tbsp flour
2/3 cup water
½ cup heavy cream

Mix sugar and flour; add beaten eggs, then water and vinegar. Cook, stirring constantly, until thick. Cool. Add heavy cream. Use over fresh or well-drained canned fruit.

Daisy Wisecarver Davis,
paternal grandmother of Donna Greeson

Cheesy Chicken and Corn Chowder

3 cups chicken broth
1 boiled whole chicken
1 can of Mexican corn
1 can of green chiles
1 can of cream of potato soup
1 pkg taco seasoning
1 small Mexican Velveeta cheese
1 8 oz sour cream

Take the chicken off the bone. Put the first six ingredients in the crock pot. Cook on low 6 to 8 hours. Mix in cheese. Stir in the sour cream. Serve with Mexican cornbread or tortilla chips.

Chili

1 ½ lb ground beef, browned
1 pkg taco seasoning
1 pkg ranch dressing
1 can dark red kidney beans
1 can chili beans
1 can diced tomatoes
1 can Rotel tomatoes

Mix all ingredients together in large pot. Bring to a boil and simmer for about 30 minutes. Serve topped with cheese, sour cream, and tortilla chips. (Can add water to thin if desired.)

George Foreman

Texan George Foreman is an Olympic Gold Medallist, two-time boxing Heavy Weight Champion, preacher, entrepreneur, and philanthropist. As an entrepreneur he has placed George Foreman's Lean Mean Grilling Machine into millions of homes around the world. He has launched numerous product lines including environmentally safe cleaning products. Foreman also focuses his energies on spending time with his family, his ministry and charitable work for the George Foreman Youth & Community Center and his "Knock-Out Pediatric Cancer" initiative among others. Visit biggeorge.com

Vanessa Channell, Ringgold Primary School

Crab Chowder

¼ tsp minced garlic
1/8 tsp cayenne
¼ cup green pepper
1 tbsp butter
2 cans potato soup
1 pkg cream cheese
1 ½ cans evaporated milk
6 oz. crab meat
1 can whole kernel corn
chopped onions
1/8 cup sugar

Cook onions, garlic, peppers, cayenne in butter. Blend in soup, cream cheese, milk. Add crab meat. Add undrained corn. Bring to boil. Reduce heat; simmer 10 minutes. Stir in sugar.

Mary Perdue First Lady of Georgia

Mary Perdue and Gov. Sonny Perdue

Perdue

As First Lady of Georgia, Mary Perdue highlighted the needs of Foster Care programs and worked to ensure children of the state are able to receive the best education possible. The First Lady and her husband, Governor Sonny Perdue, served as foster parents. Mrs. Perdue takes a stand for family and children's issues in Georgia whether the issues concern children in the public education system, in the juvenile justice system or in state custody. She was a speech pathologist in public schools and the children's ministry director in her church.

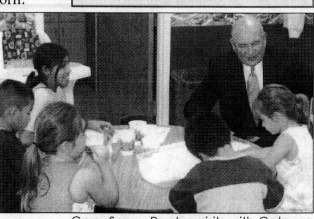

Gov. Sonny Perdue visits with Catoosa children whose parents were studying at the Catoosa County Learning Center.

ET'S Texas Troubadour Chili

**2 pounds ground beef
1 cup water
1/2 cup shortening or lard
1/2 cup chopped onions
2 tbsp minced garlic
4 tbsp chili powder
2 tbsp paprika
1/2 tsp cayenne pepper
1 tsp salt
Juice of 1 lemon
3 ounces tomato sauce**

Cook beef in a pot of cold water until it boils and meat is brown. Skim off excess grease. In a small skillet, combine enough flour and 1 cup water to make a thin paste. Cook until browned. Add to beef. Add remaining ingredients and cook slowly for 1 hour. Makes 6 to 8 servings.

*David McCormick
of Ernest Tubb Record
Shops
The Late Ernest Tubb
Country Music Artist*

Ernest Tubb

The late country music legend Ernest Tubb and his Texas Troubadours sang of a "Waltz Across Texas" and delighted the world with his self-penned "Walkin' the Floor Over You" and songs such as "Slippin' Around," "Rainbow at Midnight" and "Blue Eyed Elaine." The *Grand Ole Opry* star opened the Ernest Tubb Record Shop in Nashville and began the *Midnight Jamboree* on WSM following the *Opry* in the late 40s. Tubb's film appearances included Charles Starrett's *Fighting Buckeroos* and *Ridin' West*. Visit www.etrecordshop.com

232

Chili

1 tbsp oil
½ pound ground beef
1 small onion, chopped
1-15 oz can chili beans
(hot)
1/3 cup ketchup
1 cup water
1 tsp salt
¼ tsp pepper
¼ tsp sugar
½ tsp chili powder, or to
taste
¼ tsp cayenne pepper

(Photo: Dreama Stephenson Photography)

Heat the oil in a frying pan.
Cook the beef in the pan until
lightly brown, then push to one
side. Add the onion to the pan
and cook until soft. Drain the
excess fat. Add the remaining
ingredients and mix well.
Simmer 30 to 45 minutes. Eat
on hot dogs or in a bowl with
low-fat cheese and low-fat sour
cream. This is very good
reheated. Makes two servings,
or enough for six hot dogs.

*"Literacy is very important in
this country, without reading,
writing and being well-read our
daily lives would be effected
deeply. Having the ability to
read music, write words down to
songs and understanding their
meaning is very important in
being a musician or singer. It's
also never to late for someone
to learn these skills."*

*Larry Stephenson
Bluegrass Music Artist*

The Larry Stephenson Band

Larry Stephenson, SPBGMA
(Society for the Preservation of
Bluegrass Music in America)
Five-time Contemporary Male
Vocalist of the Year, is a mem-
ber of the Virginia Country Music
Hall of Fame. The Larry
Stephenson Band, which
includes Larry, Kyle Perkins,
Kenny Ingram, and Kevin
Richardson entertains audiences
from coast to coast. In 2008 he
received the IBMA's "Recorded
Event of the Year" award for
participating on Everett Lilly's
CD. His band was nominated in
2008 for Gospel Album of the
Year in the Independent Music
Awards for *Thankful*, with guests
Sonya Isaacs and Missy Raines.
Visit
www.LarryStephensonBand.com

Creamy Pumpkin Corn Chowder

3 cups chicken broth (from bouillon cubes)
1 tbsp olive oil
¼ cup leeks, fresh, sliced 1/8" (substitute 2 green onions)
¼ cup carrots, fresh, diced
2 lb chopped potatoes
6 oz. canned pumpkin (mashed)
10 oz heavy whipping cream (substitute: 5 oz. milk)
½ cup corn, frozen, thawed, drained
2 tsp parsley leaves, fresh, chopped
Salt to taste
Cayenne pepper to taste
¼ tsp ground cloves

Prepare chicken broth. In a large soup kettle, sauté leeks and carrots in oil until tender. Add broth. Bring to a boil. Add potatoes. Cook until tender. Combine pumpkin and small amount of hot broth. Whisk until smooth. Stir back into soup. Stir in cream and corn. Simmer for 10 to 15 minutes. Stir in parsley, salt, pepper, and cloves.
Joanne Ritchie

Crockpot Beef Stew

1 ½ to 2 lbs beef stew meat cut into 1 inch cubes
1/8 cup flour
½ tsp salt
½ tsp pepper
1 ½ cups beef broth
1 tsp Worcestershire sauce
1 clove garlic, minced
1 tsp paprika
4 shiitake mushrooms or 1 pkg regular mushrooms, sliced
2 carrots sliced
2 medium potatoes, diced
1 onion, chopped
1 stalk celery, chopped

Put beef in crock-pot. Mix together the flour, salt and pepper and pour over the meat, stirring to coat each piece of meat with flour. Add the remaining ingredients and stir to mix well. Cover and cook on low for 10-12 hours or on high for 4-6 hours.
Cindie Robinson, Uniktings

> The man who doesn't read good books has no advantage over the man who can't read them.
> *Mark Twain*

The highest result of education is tolerance.
Helen Keller

Helen Keller

Longtime Catoosa County teacher Euphie Deverell Center remembers Helen Keller visiting Catoosa County early one morning in 1928 along with a companion. Keller appeared as a guest speaker while Euphie was attending Ringgold High School. As a result of meningitis, Keller lost her sight and hearing as a baby. With the assistance of teacher Anne Sullivan, Keller found her way through the darkness to become one of the first blind and deaf persons to effectively communicate. It was probably Anne Sullivan who traveled with her to Ringgold. Keller became an international celebrity, writing, speaking and working for the betterment of others. In this photo Keller poses with writer Mark Twain circa 1899.

(Photo courtesy the Helen Keller Foundation)

235

ORIENTATION

Cleo's Vegetable Beef Soup

1 large soup pot with lid or large crock-pot with lid.
1-3 lbs beef cubes
1-2 cans (48oz) V-8 Juice
1 bunch of fresh green onions, chopped
1 big round onion whole, washed, but not cut up or chopped
7-9 very small new potatoes, chopped into bite size cubes
1 head broccoli
1-3 cans mixed vegetables
1-3 cans corn, field peas, black-eyed peas, green beans, carrots, new potatoes
(Best if fresh vegetables are used)
Onion powder, to taste
Seasoning salt, to taste
Lemon pepper, to taste

Season the meat with onion powder, seasoning salt and lemon pepper, then brown on all sides. You will need to do this with a pot or pan on the stove. Add chopped green onions with a little water, just enough to cover the beef cubes, also in the same pan. Let boil for 25-30 minutes or so on high, add water if needed. Transfer to crock-pot if you desire.

Add V8 juice (enough to fill pot 1/3 full). Add vegetables (not broccoli, yet). Cut the whole onion in half and drop 1 half in the soup. Cook on high and add enough V8 juice to cover vegetables. Be careful not to fill it too full, leave room for bubbling. Add lid.

After two hours or so cut down the heat to simmer and let cook for at least 2 more hours. After 2 ½ hours add broccoli. Remember to stir often.

Other things can make it great:
Grilling the meat first
Using beef broth along with V8
Using fresh, washed vegetables
Adding other spices along with the other ones

Enjoy!!!

Tom Drenon, Drummer for country artist Darryl Worley

Creamy Potato Soup

5-6 potatoes
Water
1 small onion
1 can corn, or 1 small bag of frozen corn (optional)
1/3 cup butter or margarine
1 can cream of chicken soup
1 can cream of mushroom soup
1 (8oz) brick of cream cheese (or Neufchatel cheese)
½ cup milk
Hot sauce (I use 4-5 drips, but use at your discretion)

Peel and chop up potatoes. Chop onion. Boil potatoes and onion in water until fork tender (you can also use one can of chicken broth and then water, but either way, use just enough liquid to cover the potatoes) once fork tender reduce heat to medium high. Add 1/3 cup butter/margarine and corn and stir together. Add cream of chicken soup and then add cream of mushroom. Cook for about five minutes stirring consistently to mix together. Cut cream cheese brick into about 8-12 sections and add to soup. Let this cook stirring consistently until cream cheese has melted and mixed into soup. Add hot sauce and salt and pepper to taste.

Jackie Goolsby,
Georgia Department of Labor, Northwest Georgia Career Center

Jackie Goolsby, CCL Task Force member

Goolsby

Position: Employer Marketing Representative
Business: Georgia Department of Labor
Reason for serving on the task force: To ensure I inform the Catoosa county residents and employers about the services provided by the Learning Center. I also include the surrounding counties of the benefits the Learning Center offers.
Organizations: Catoosa Chamber, Catoosa Chamber Ambassador, Walker Chamber, Dade Chamber, and Catoosa Family Collaborative
Favorite Movie: *O' Brother Where Art Thou*
Favorite Book: *This Present Darkness*
Favorite Quote: "People may not remember what you did or what you said, but they will always remember how you made them feel."

Barbara Bush and Former President George Bush

In 1989, former First Lady Barbara Bush developed the Barbara Bush Foundation for Family Literacy, an organization that fosters the cre-

ation of literacy programs around the country. Mrs. Bush stressed the importance of reading aloud to children by regu- larly appearing on *Mrs. Bush's Story Time*, a national radio program. In addition to her best-selling autobi- ography *Barbara Bush: A Memoir*, Mrs. Bush authored *C. Fred's Story* and the best-selling *Millie's Book*, both of whose profits benefited the literacy cause.

Gazpacho

2 cups beef bouillon
2 cloves garlic
1/3-1/2 cup fresh lemon juice
¼ cup extra virgin olive oil
1 tbsp paprika
1 tbsp salt or to taste
1 tsp freshly ground black pepper or to taste
18 oz tomato juice
4 cups tomatoes (about 8 fresh)
1 green pepper, coarsely chopped
¾-1 cup chopped onion
1 cup chopped cucumber, (unwaxed and seeded)

Place all liquid and season- ings plus one-half of all the vegetables (except the green pepper) into food processor and puree. Place in large pitcher.
Coarsely chop the rest of the ingredients (including all of the green pepper) by hand or processor. Add to the gazpacho mix. Tabasco may be added to taste. Makes one gallon and keeps up to two weeks chilled. Crab meat may be added at the last minute.
For that special occasion in Maine, I use lobster.

Barbara Bush
Former First Lady
of the United States
& Former President George H.W. Bush

Loobyie – Green Bean-Meat Stew

2 tbsp olive oil
1 large onion chopped
1 ½ lbs lean lamb or beef stew
meat, cut into small cubes
Water
2 lbs trimmed green beans or
pole beans
1 can (1lb 12oz) tomatoes,
undrained and chopped
1 can (8oz) tomato sauce
1 tomato sauce can of water
Salt, to taste
Pepper, to taste
½ tsp cinnamon

Heat oil in large, heavy saucepan. Sauté onion in oil until limp and transparent. Add lamb or beef cubes and sauté until meat is brown. Add water to cover meat. Bring to boil, reduce heat and simmer, covered until meat is tender, about one hour. Stir in beans, tomatoes and their juice, tomato sauce, water and seasonings. Mix together very well. Bring to a boil, reduce heat and simmer, covered, until the beans are tender and the sauce is thick. I serve this over rice for a great one dish meal.

Vince and Barbara Dooley

The mixture of football and the University of Georgia mean only one thing for many Georgians, that is College Football Hall of Famer Vince Dooley. One of the most winningest coaches in history, Dooley led the Georgia Bulldogs to 201 victories as head coach and took Bulldog teams to 20 bowl games. His wife Barbara is an author, radio and television personality and career woman who also shares her talents as a speaker. She is co-host the cooking show *Dixie Divas in the Kitchen* for Georgia Public Television with Ronda Rich Visit barbaraandvincedooley.com

This is a dish that we eat a lot during Lent when we are cutting down on meat or fasting.
Vince and Barbara Dooley

Mac and Cheese Soup

1 (14 oz) macaroni noodles
2 ½ cups milk
1 cup broccoli
1 can cream cheddar cheese soup
½ c chopped onion
1 cup ham (cooked)
1 cup water

Cook macaroni according to the package directions; drain. (do not stir in the package of cheese that comes with the macaroni yet) In medium saucepan combine broccoli, onion, and water. Bring to boil and cook until broccoli is tender. Stir in macaroni, cheese mixture from the package, milk, soup and ham. Return to a boil briefly. Serve.

Vanessa Channell, Ringgold Primary School

Mama Evie's Chili

1-2 lbs ground beef
1 tsp margarine
1 onion, chopped
2 tsp sugar, divided
Salt and Pepper to taste
1 pkg Chili-O seasoning
1 jar (24oz) picante sauce
1 can (28oz) diced tomatoes
3 cans beans, your choice (I use 2 pinto and 1 red kidney)

Brown ground beef in margarine in skillet. Add chopped onion, salt, pepper, and 1 tsp sugar. When browned, put in large pot and add chili-o seasoning and stir. Add picante sauce, tomatoes, and remaining sugar. Mix in beans. Let simmer. Serve with crackers or cornbread.

Joy Thornton

Oh, So Simple (but tasty) Stew

1 can French Onion soup
1 can Golden Mushroom soup
1 lb beef tips

Mix soups together in crockpot. Add meat. Cook for approximately 4 hours on Low or 2 hours on high.

Vanessa Channell, Ringgold Primary School

Shoney's ® Cabbage Soup

1 head cabbage, coarsely chopped and steamed
1 large onion, chopped
3 bell peppers, chopped
½ to 1 lb ground round
2 cans (16 oz) dark red kidney beans
1 tsp salt
1 tsp sugar
1 tsp pepper
1 container (46oz) V-8 juice
1 pkg dry onion soup mix

Saute onion, bell pepper and ground beef together, drain off any fat. In soup pot, combine kidney beans, salt, pepper, sugar, V-8 juice, onion soup mix. Add cabbage and meat mixture. Cook at low simmer for about two hours stirring often. Delicious with cornbread and cold milk. Makes about 6 quarts and freezes well. Recipe from Chattanooga Times Free Press, Nov. 1994.

Norma Haisten

Spicy Tomato Soup

Serves: 4-6

1 tbsp olive oil
1 ½ cups minced onion
3-4 cloves garlic, minced or crushed
½ tsp salt
1 tbsp fresh dill (or more to taste)
Freshly ground black pepper
1 can (1lb, 12oz) crushed tomatoes
2 cups water
1 tbsp honey
2 medium fresh tomatoes, diced

Heat olive oil in a kettle. Add onion, garlic, salt, dill, and black pepper. Stir over medium heat for about 5-8 minutes, or until the onions are translucent. Add crushed tomatoes, water and honey. Cover and simmer over low heat for 20 minutes. About 5 minutes before serving, stir in fresh tomatoes. Serve hot, topped with fresh herbs.

Ed Begley
Actor

> *Reading is essential for success in this world.*
> **Ed Begley**

Ed Begley, Jr.

Ed Begley Jr. is a second-generation actor who first endeared himself into the American experience through his role as Dr. Victor Ehrlich on *St. Elsewhere*. His talents keep him in demand for roles in films such as *Pineapple Express*, *A Mighty Wind*, *Batman Forever* and *The In-Laws*. He often appears in recurring roles on popular TV shows such as *Seventh Heaven*, *Boston Legal*, and *Six Feet Under*. Begley is an active environmental advocate giving his time to many organizations that strive to protect our environment.

Visit www.edbegley.com

Taco Soup

1 lb ground beef
2 cans pinto beans
2 cans corn
1 can petite diced tomatoes
1 pkg taco seasoning
Salt, to taste
Pepper, to taste
1 bag Doritos
1 container sour cream
1 bag shredded Mexican style cheese

Brown and drain ground beef. Add pinto beans, corn, tomatoes and taco seasoning. Salt and pepper to taste. Bring to a boil. Serve hot. Place toppings (Doritos, sour cream and cheese) to the side to add when served.

Wendy Brownfield

Tommy's "Like a Vegan" Soup

1 can black beans
1 can vegetable broth
1 small can Mexicorn
1 can diced tomatoes and chiles
½ cup salsa
1 tbsp fresh cut cilantro

Combine all ingredients except cilantro in a saucepan and heat until piping hot. When hot, add cilantro to soup and stir. Serve with tortilla chips or flour tortillas.

Tommy Housworth

Vince Dooley's Pumpkin Soup

Serves: 10-12

1 large sweet onion
1 tbsp olive oil
1 tbsp minced garlic
1 tbsp minced fresh ginger
1/8 tsp ground red pepper
1/8 tsp ground cumin
2 cans (15oz) unsweetened pumpkin
1 cup water
1 container (32oz) low-sodium fat free chicken broth
1 ½ cup half and half milk
2 tbsp fresh lime juice
2 ½ tsp salt

Combine all ingredients and let simmer for 40 minutes.
Garnish with sour cream and fresh chives. For a more elegant
dish, top this soup with cooked crab meat or cooked shrimp.

Vince and Barbara Dooley

The Little General Family and Children's Park in Ringgold features a theme centered around the Great Locomotive Chase and provides recreation opportunities for families with younger children. (Photo by Randall Franks)

White Chili

2 tbsp vegetable oil
1 medium onion, finely chopped
1 can chopped green chilis
2 tsp garlic powder
2 tsp oregano
2 tsp cumin
2 tsp cilantro (optional)
2 tsp salt
½ tsp cayenne pepper (optional, depending on how spicy you want it)
2 cans Northern beans (total around 40 ounces)
2 ½ cups chicken broth
Chicken cooked and diced (about 4 breasts or 2-3 cans of chicken)

The Florida monument at Chickamauga Battlefield
(Photo by Randall Franks)

Brown onions in oil, add chilis and spices. Stir well. In large pot, add above and remaining ingredients. Bring to boil. Let cool.Tastes best if place in fridge overnight but can serve immediately. Top with cheese.
*add more/less chicken broth to chili, depending upon how thick you like it.

Vanessa Channell, Ringgold Primary School

Extra Curriculum
(Vegetables & Side Dishes)

Carol Burnett

Carol Burnett brought joy to millions each week on her television show *The Carol Burnett Show*. The show aired on CBS from 1967-1978 including a cast featuring Tim Conway, Vicki Lawrence, Harvey Korman, Lyle Wagonner and others. Burnett began her work on Broadway in *Once Upon a Mattress* and then made appearances on *The Garry Moore Show*. Through the years since leaving her popular variety show, she shares her talents in special appearances on numerous films and TV shows including *Mama's Family*, *Mad About You*, *Law and Order: Special Victims Unit*, *Desperate Housewives*, and *All My Children* and even as "Kangaroo" in the animated feature *Horton Hears a Who*.

Amazingly Goode Okra

24 medium size okras
2 tbsp butter
1 medium minced onion
1 medium minced green pepper
2 raw peeled tomatoes
3 tbsp chili sauce
salt
pepper
garlic

(© 2003 Randall Franks, photo by Lynn Lockwood)

Randall Franks, David Hart and Alan Autry pause while filming on the Sparta Police Department set in the *In the Heat of the Night* soundstage in Covington, Georgia.

Wash the okras well in cold water. Drain and cut off both ends. Place them in a saucepan of boiling salted water and cook for 15 minutes. Lift out with a skimmer and drain on a cloth. In a frying pan place the butter, onion and green pepper. Sauté for six minutes until onion and green pepper are golden.

Cut the tomatoes into fine bits and add to the frying pan along with chili sauce. Season with salt, pepper and a little garlic to taste if you like. Add okra to the frying pan and cook slowly for 15 minutes. Turn the ingredients into a hot deep dish for serving and sprinkle with chopped parsley.

Randall Franks,
Actor/Appalachian & Southern
Gospel Music Artist;
CCL Taskforce Past Chairman

Randall Franks

While appearing as "Officer Randy Goode" on the CBS and NBC series *In the Heat of the Night*, Randall Franks used his down-home, boy-next-door appeal to speak to thousands of youth in schools across the country encouraging them to live a drug-free life. Known as the "Appalachian Ambassador of the Fiddle," the award-winning singer, musician, writer and photographer is a top-selling Southern Gospel music artist who performs his unique style of music and comedy at fairs and festivals around the country. Among Franks' films are *Firebase 9, Phoenix Falling, Desperate for Love* and *The Flamingo Rising* from "Hallmark Hall of Fame." Visit www.myspace.com/randallfranksmusic

Boiled Peanuts

1 ½ quarts raw uncooked peanuts
½ cup salt
2 ½ quarts water
Wash peanuts until water runs clear. Put clean peanuts in
Crockpot. Add salt and water; stir. Cook covered, on high for 5
to 7 hours. Add more water, if necessary, to keep peanuts covered.

Jill Van Dyke, Catoosa County Health Department

The Ringgold Wedding Chapel

Ringgold is Georgia's Wedding Capital and many celebrities are
among the thousands of ceremonies on record. American icon Dolly
Parton said the name of the town reminded her of rings of gold and
that drew her to marry here at the First Baptist Church of Ringgold.
Country Music Hall of Famer Tammy Wynette married twice in cere-
monies at the Catoosa County Courthouse to two fellow entertainers
Don Chapel and George Jones. Even Louisiana Governor Jimmie
Davis brought his sunshine Anna Carter Gordon of gospel music's
Chuck Wagon Gang to marry here at the Ringgold United Methodist
Church. The original building now serves as the Ringgold Wedding
Chapel where even today's stars and folks from around the region

Broccoli Casserole

2 (10 oz) pkg. frozen broccoli
1 chopped onion
2 cups cooked rice
1 small jar Cheez Whiz
1 stick butter
1 can cream of chicken soup
Cheez-its

Preheat oven 350°. Cook broccoli by directions on package. Drain. Cook rice in the meantime. Sauté onions in butter until tender. In bowl, mix sautéed onions, Cheez Whiz, and cream of chicken soup until creamy. Mix broccoli and rice with this mixture. Mix well. Put in casserole dish. Crush Cheez-its and put on top. Cook in a 350° oven for 15 to 20 minutes.

Vanessa Channell, Ringgold Primary School

Broccoli Medley

1 tbsp olive oil
1 clove garlic, minced
1 ¼ lb. broccoli, cut in bite-size pieces (5 cups)
½ red pepper, cut in thin strips
½ yellow pepper, cut in thin strips
2 tbsp soy sauce

Heat olive oil and garlic in wok or skillet. Add broccoli and stir-fry for 1 minute. Add peppers and continue to stir-fry for 3 to 4 minutes more or until vegetables are crisp-tender. Add soy sauce. Cook and stir until heated through.

Corn Casserole

3 cans corn, drained
2 pkgs cream cheese, softened
2 sticks butter or margarine
1 sleeve Ritz crackers, crushed

Melt margarine and mix with cream cheese. Fold in corn. Put in glass baking dish. Bake at 350° for 10-15 minutes. Add crushed Ritz crackers, dot with butter, bake for 10 minutes longer or until crackers are browned.

Dusty Nichols Murphy

Corn Pudding
Serves: 8

1 can (14.75oz) creamed corn
1 can (15.25oz) whole corn, drained
1 (8 ½ oz) package corn muffin mix
1 (8 oz) container sour cream
¼ cup butter or margarine
3 eggs, beaten

Combine all ingredients in a large bowl. Pour into a lightly greased 11x7" pan. Bake at 350° for one hour.

Frances Holsinger,
Reading Student

Rue McClanahan

Rue McClanahan walked into living rooms playing a villainous character on the soap opera *Another World* in 1970 after several years of thrilling audiences from the stage and some film roles. However, it was as "Maude's" best friend "Vivian Harmon" played opposite Bea Arthur in the 1970s series *Maude* and later her "Blanche Devereaux" on the *The Golden Girls* (1985-92) with Arthur, Betty White, and Estelle Getty that endeared her to audiences and solidified her place in TV history. She won four nominations and an Emmy ® for playing "Blanche." She continues appearance in television and film roles recently appearing in the series *Law and Order, Sordid Lives: The Series.*

Curly's Broccoli and Rice Casserole

10 oz frozen chopped broccoli
1 medium onion, chopped
½ cup uncooked rice
¾ stick margarine
1-10 ¾ oz can of cream of mush-
room soup
salt and pepper to taste
grated cheese

Put the broccoli and onions in a pot and cook according to the directions on the package, then drain. In another pot, cook the rice for at least 10 minutes or according to package directions. Combine broccoli, rice, margarine, and soup. Add a little milk if mixture is too thick. Add salt and pepper to taste. Pour into a greased Pyrex dish and sprinkle the top with grated cheese. Bake at 350 degrees for 20 to 30 minutes. Makes about 4 servings
Curly Seckler
Bluegrass Music Artist

Curly Seckler

Bluegrass tenor Curly Seckler helped to form one of the classic sounds in Bluegrass after joining the Flatt and Scruggs' Foggy Mountain Boys. Their unique sound resulted when his voice was paired with Lester Flatt's voice and the banjo work of Earl Scruggs. Seckler also contributed to the sounds of Jim and Jesse, Charlie Monroe and Ramblin' Tommy Scott, among others. In the 1970s, he rejoined Lester Flatt in his Nashville Grass. After Flatt's death, Seckler led the group, which included Marty Stuart.
Visit www.curlyseckler.net

Curly Seckler (right) appearing with Lester Flatt and Earl Scruggs and the Foggy Mountain Boys.

"Doc Robb's" Southern Casserole

1 cup uncooked grits
1 tsp salt
4 cup water
1 stick of margarine or butter
1/4 lb Velveeta cheese
1/4 lb sharp cheese, grated
3 eggs, slightly beaten
1/3 cup milk

Cook grits in 4 cups of salted water. Add margarine, cheeses, eggs and milk. Stir until cheese is melted and smooth. Place in a casserole dish and bake for one hour at 325 to 350 degrees.

Dan Biggers
Actor

Dan Biggers

A real-life former college dean, Dan Biggers has television and film credits spanning two decades. In 1988, he reached national attention after landing the role of kindly "Doc" Robb on the hit series *In the Heat of the Night*. In 1999, Biggers played his only on-screen role as a teacher and priest in the film *Passing Glory* with actor Rip Torn. Some of his other notable films and television appearances include *Savannah, I'll Fly Away, Matlock, Glory, Paris Trout, Queen* and *To Dance with the White Dog*.

"Doc" Tommy Scott's Medicine Show Delight

1 can Pork 'n Beans
1 clove minced garlic
1 rib celery, finely chopped
1 bay leaf
1/2 medium onion, diced
dash Tabasco
1 tsp. maple syrup

Sauté onion, garlic and celery till softened. Add remaining ingredients and stir to mix well. Bake 350 degrees approx. 30 minutes. Makes 3 to 4 small side servings. Please note: The "Doc" did not add any "Snake Oil."

Ramblin' Doc Tommy Scott Country Music Artist/Actor

(Photos courtesy Tommy Scott)

Ramblin' "Doc" Tommy Scott

Step right up and get you a bottle of Snake Oil! Beginning on "Doc" Chamberlain's medicine show for just $6 a week, Ramblin' "Doc" Tommy Scott's career has spanned into nine decades. Scott parlayed his musical and comedic talent, along with Chamberlain's retirement gift of the medicine formulas, into a lifelong calling. Over 29,000 live performances later, he is still going. In the 1940s he joined the *Grand Ole Opry* starring with the classic cast of Roy Acuff, Minnie Pearl and Uncle Dave Macon. In films, he played the mountaineer in projects like *Mountain Capers* and *Hoboes and Indians* and the singing cowboy in Edward Dmytryk's *Trail of the Hawk*. On television, he starred in two series of his own, *The Ramblin' Tommy Scott Show* and *Smokey Mountain Jamboree*. He has also appeared in shows ranging from *That's Incredible* to *Extreme Homes* and with everyone from Johnny Carson to Oprah Winfrey. With around 500 recordings to his credit and dozens of popular singles, "Rosebuds and You" is probably the biggest career hit for Scott. Visit TommyScott.net

Glorified Hashbrowns

**2 (10 ¾ oz) cans cream of celery soup, undiluted
2 (8 oz.) chive and onion cream cheese
1 (2 lb) pkg frozen cubed hash brown potatoes
1 cup (4 oz) shredded cheddar cheese**

In large microwave-safe bowl, combine soup and cream cheese. Cover and cook on high for 3-4 minutes or until cream cheese is melted, stirring occasionally. Add potatoes and stir until coated. Spoon into greased 13x9x2 inch baking dish. Bake uncovered at 350° for 35-40 minutes or until potatoes are tender. Sprinkle with cheddar cheese and bake 3-5 minutes longer or until cheese is melted.

Why Literacy is Important to Me:
Because along with work, laughter, and love, it spells success!

Mary Lou Retton
Olympic Gymnast

Mary Lou Retton

(GED recipient)

In 1984, when Mary Lou Retton became the first and only American to win the Olympic All-Around Gold Medal in gymnastics, she took home five medals and entered the hearts of people all over the U.S. One national survey named her "America's Most Popular Athlete." Today as a motivational speaker and corporate spokesperson, she travels the world as a Fitness Ambassador promoting the benefits of proper nutrition and regular exercise.
Visit www.marylouretton.com

EXTRA CURRICULUM

Doug Dillard

Douglas Dillard as "Jebbin Darling" rode into the fabric of American culture in the back of Briscoe Darling's truck when he and his Darling brothers and sister Charlene came down from the hills into Mayberry to give Andy Taylor, Barney Fife and all the town folks on the *Andy Griffith Show* a ride they would never forget. Denver Pyle, who played Briscoe Darling, joined Andy Griffith and Don Knotts, who played Sheriff Taylor and Deputy Fife. The Darling sister and brothers were played by Maggie Peterson and The Dillards: Doug, banjo; Rodney, guitar; Mitch Jayne, bass; and Dean Webb, mandolin. Through his portrayal of Jebbin Darling and countless studio recordings, film soundtracks, movie roles and live appearances, the IBMA Bluegrass Hall of Famer become one of music's most influential banjo stylists. Visit hollywoodhillbilly.com/ dougdillard/

A Darling's Dish of Beans

1 pound of dried navy or great northern beans
4 strips of swine (bacon)
1 tsp of salt
2 cups of chopped ham of hog

Before you get started cookin', you need to remove all the rotten beans, rocks, dirt and foreign beans. Wash each bean individually with a toothbrush until there is not one single solitary speck of dirt left on them. Boil the beans once in pure water for 2 minutes. While waitin' fry 4 strips of swine until almost crisp. Take the beans off the flame, drain, rinse them with hot water, so as to put them into shock and cause them to jump out of their skins. Put the beans in clean hot water on a low flame. Render the grease and add fried swine to the beans. Add 1 teaspoon of salt and chopped ham. Cook on a low flame for about 2 hours. The beans should not be overcooked as the soup will have the consistency of library paste. The bean broth should be fairly clear while the beans should be firm and not cooked to death. If you do not like white beans, give em a try. Remember eatin' speaks louder than words. You never know you may even her your darling say "Good Beans."

Douglas Dillard
Actor/Bluegrass Music
Artist

Douglas Dillard and Andy Griffith share a laugh on the set of *The Andy Griffith Show*

Grilled Veggies ala Richmond

Eggplant
Red & green peppers
Broccoli
Asparagus
Squash (whatever is in season) (Check out your local veggie stand and see what appeals to you…most veggies that are solid (not leafy will work.)

Branscombe Richmond visits the Crazy Horse Memorial located in the Black Hills of South Dakota. The work was begun in 1948 by sculptor Korczak Ziolkowski at the request of Native Americans. Following Korczak death in 1982, his wife Ruth and their family continue the project working with the Crazy Horse Memorial Foundation.

Cut vegetables into chunks/slices about 4"x4". For the asparagus, the trick is to bend the rough end until it breaks naturally. That way you have just the most edible part of the stalk. Pour enough high grade virgin olive oil over the vegetables and make sure that they are well covered in oil. Let them marinate for a half hour. Cook them over medium to hot coals until they are al dente or you can put a fork in them fairly easily. Do not overcook because they will get soggy. Eat right away. These are also good for leftovers the next day…they are easy to microwave and have with your leftover meats.

In our house, the most favorite meals are the ones we cook out on the grill. With all the health notices on eating too much meat, we've found that most of our favorite vegetables grill spectacularly! And because we live in California, we can grill year round! The secret is that olive oil is known to be one of the best oils for your health and it seems to bring out the natural flavors in the veggies for a lip smackin' meal.

Branscombe Richmond, Actor/Music Artist

Branscombe Richmond

Branscombe Richmond is best known as Bobby Sixkiller, a bounty hunter on the hit television series *Renegade* in which he co-starred with Lorenzo Lamas. He can now be seen on the new series *Tremors*. The actor, director and entertainer has logged over 300 hours on television and 100 motion pictures including *Batman Returns, Hard to Kill, Commando, License to Kill* and *Star Trek III*. He recently co-starred in *The Scorpion King* with WWF champion "The Rock." In addition to serving as the national spokesperson for Indian Motorcycles, Richmond is currently starring in *Destiny*, which also stars Mickey Rourke, Casper Van Dien, Theresa Russell and William Forsythe. He tours the world singing with his band, Branscombe Richmond & The Renegade Posse.

Visit www.branscomberichmond.com

Mujadarra (Lentils)

1 cup lentils, washed
1 tsp salt
4 cups water
4 tbsp olive oil
1 large onion, chopped
fine
¼ cup rice
1/3 tsp pepper

Cook lentils in water over
medium heat for about 20
minutes. In the meantime,
sauté the onions in oil
until lightly browned and
add to the lentils. Add rice
and seasonings and cook
for about 15-20 minutes
or until rice is done.

*Vince and Barbara
Dooley*

Music and movie star
Bing Crosby visited
Catoosa County during the
World War II to perform for the
WAAC's stationed
at Fort Oglethorpe.
(Courtesy 6th Cavalry
Museum)

Oven Roasted Asparagus

3 lbs fresh asparagus
3 garlic cloves, minced
2 tbsp olive oil
¾ tsp salt
½ tsp ground black pepper
½ cup slivered almonds, toasted

Snap off and discard tough ends of the asparagus; place
asparagus on lightly greased baking sheet. Drizzle evenly with
olive oil; sprinkle evenly with garlic salt, and pepper. Bake at
350° for 10 minutes or to desired tenderness. Transfer to serving dish; sprinkle with almonds.

Vanessa Channell, Ringgold Primary School

Grilled Asparagus with Spicy Ranch Dressing

1 cup light mayo or sour cream
¼ tsp red pepper flakes
¼ cup buttermilk
1 envelope buttermilk ranch dressing mix
¼ cup red onion, chopped
1 tbsp chopped fresh basil
3 tbsp lemon juice, divided
2 lb fresh asparagus
1/8 tsp salt
1/8 tsp pepper

For dressing: Whisk together mayo (sour cream), buttermilk, dressing mix, onion, basil, 1 tbsp lemon juice, and pepper flakes. Cover and chill.
Snap off tough ends of asparagus and remove scales with a vegetable peeler, if desired. Pour 1 tbsp lemon juice over asparagus and sprinkle with salt and pepper.
Place asparagus on grill rack coated with nonstick cooking spray and grill, uncovered, over medium heat 10 minutes or until asparagus is tender, turning if needed. Remove from grill and drizzle remaining tablespoon of lemon juice over asparagus. Serve with Spicy Ranch dressing.

Hot Boiled Cabbage

1 large cabbage (about 2 1/2 lb.), cut into bite-size pieces
2 green tomatoes, chopped
1 large green bell pepper, chopped
1 cup water
1/3 cup hot pickled banana peppers, chopped
1 tablespoon vegetable oil
1 teaspoon salt
1/2 teaspoon pepper

Bring all ingredients to a boil in a large nonstick skillet over medium-high heat. Cover, reduce heat, and simmer, stirring occasionally, 25 minutes or until cabbage is tender.

Vanessa Channell, Ringgold Primary School

Oven-Roasted Vegetables

1 lb sweet potatoes
Asparagus spears
3 large carrots, cut in 1" pieces
2 medium onions, cut and quartered
1 large green pepper
1 medium red pepper
Mushrooms, sliced
Eggplant, cleaned and cut in 1-2" pieces
2 tbsp olive or vegetable oil
Cavender's Greek seasoning

Preheat oven to 400°. Arrange vegetables attractively after spraying them with cooking spray. In roasting pan, toss vegetables with oil and herbs. Roast 1 hour until tender, stirring occasionally.

Grace Davis, Parent Involvement Coordinator Catoosa County Schools

Potato Casserole

1 bag frozen hash brown potatoes
1 large container sour cream
1 can cream of chicken soup
1 medium onion diced
Longhorn cheese, shredded
Salt, to taste
Pepper, to taste

Mix all ingredients. Bake uncovered 350° for about 10 minutes or until bubbling.

Roberta Boyd

Spicy Mashed Sweet Potatoes with Maple Syrup

6 lbs fresh sweet potatoes, scrubbed and clean)
1/3 to ½ cup of good quality maple syrup
4 tsp pureed canned chipotle chiles, adjust for desired heat
¾ cup sour cream or plain yogurt
1 ½ tsp ground cinnamon
Salt to taste

Cook sweet potatoes until soft in a microwave, by boiling, or by baking at 375° for up to one hour. Combine syrup, sour cream, chipotle puree, cinnamon and salt in a small bowl. Whisk until smooth. After potatoes are cooked and soft, remove the peel and pass through a potato ricer, food mill or potato masher. Blend in other ingredients with a rubber spatula to combine. Taste for seasoning and transfer to a warm serving bowl. Serve immediately.

Former First Lady Laura Bush

Professor Bryan's School meets at the Masonic Literary Institute building in Ringgold around 1916. Students are (from left, first row) Reo Bandy, Ethel Robertson, Kattie Trimier, Hazel Shell, May White, Gladys Henry, Erma Watts, Emma Clark, (second row) Birdie Horne, Delia Bandy, Tommy Edwards, Pearl Black, Jewel Whittle, Ruth Carroll, Alice Cotter, Hattie Denman, Eva Henry, (third row) Nell Broaderick, Nina Bates, Grace England, Edna Keith, Maude Keith, Fannie Glass and Bernice White.

(Photo courtesy The Catoosa County Historical Society)

Sweet Potato Souffle

3 cups
sweet pota-
toes cooked
1 teaspoon
vanilla
1 cup sugar
1 egg
1/4 cup milk
3 tablespoons flour
1/2 cup margarine or butter
1 teaspoon cinnamon

Melt margarine or butter. Mash sweet potatoes. Mix all ingredients with potatoes and place in buttered baking dish.

Topping
1 1/3 cup brown sugar
1/3 cup plain flour
1 cup coconut (optional)
1/2 stick margarine or butter
1 cup chopped nuts
mix and crumble on top
Melt margarine or butter. Mix ingredients in a bowl and and spread over top. Bake at 325 degrees for 45 minutes.
The Watkins Family
Bluegrass Gospel Artists

The Watkins Family

The Watkins Family includes matriarch Judy Watkins and her three adult children Todd, Lorie and Shanon. They continue a path sharing their love of Jesus through traditional music touring across the United States and Canada since 1982. Their latest project is "Heaven's Worth Waiting For." Lorie was nominated twice as Female Vocalist of the Year in the Front Porch Fellowship Bluegrass Gospel Music Awards. She appeared in the National Quartet Convention All-Star Band in 2008 and 2009.
The group has shared concert stages performing for thousands beside acts such a Randy Travis and Diamond Rio. The Watkins Family have received nominations as Best Bluegrass Act at the Coca-Cola Music Awards previously hosted in Atlanta.
Visit
www.watkinsfamilymusic.com

J eff Carson

Jeff Carson rode "The Car" to the top of the charts in 1995 and to a win for ACM Video of the Year. As a songwriter, Kenny Rogers recorded his "Until Forever's Gone," a song Carson wrote with Jim Weatherly. Carson's Curb CD, Real Life, featured the single "Until We Fall Back In Love Again." Carson is a real-life police officer in Franklin, Tenn.
Visit www.jeffcarson.net.

Summer Squash Casserole

2 lbs squash
1 cup grated cheddar cheese
2 eggs, beaten
1 tsp ground sage
1 medium onion, chopped
1 tbsp sugar
1 tbsp butter
 salt, pepper to taste
paprika for topping, to taste

Cut squash into bite size pieces and steam for 20 minutes, until tender. Combine all ingredients, except ½ of cheese and paprika. Top with remaining cheese and paprika. Bake at 350° for 25 minutes. Bake in 9x9 Pyrex dish, and do not over bake or dish will become dry. Enjoy

Jeff & Kim Carson
Country Music Artist

The Kentucky monument at Chickamauga Battlefield
(Photo by Randall Franks)

Western Bean Bake

1 lb hamburger
1 lb bacon
1 onion, chopped
½ cup catsup
½ cup barbecue sauce
1 tsp salt
1 tbsp prepared mustard
4 tbsp molasses
1 tsp chili powder
2 (16 oz) cans red kidney beans
¾ tsp pepper
2 (16 oz) cans pork and beans
2 (16 oz) cans butter, navy or pea beans

Brown hamburger and onions and drain off fat. Cook bacon and drain on paper towel. Add to rest of ingredients and mix. Bake 1 hour at 350°, or may be done in crock pot. Start crock pot on high for an hour then turn to low and cook several hours. Check, and if too dry, add a little water.

Jeannie Seely
Country Music Artist

Monte Hale

Monte Hale (1919-2009)rode and sang his way into the hearts of American youth in the Saturday matinees of the 1940s. He starred in 19 Republic films in four years. Some among those films are *Man from Rainbow Valley, Out California Way,* and *Under Colorado Skies.* In supporting roles he worked in *Giant* with James Dean, Rock Hudson, and Elizabeth Taylor, and *The Chase* with Robert Redford and Marlon Brando. Gunsmoke and Wells Fargo were among his TV roles. He appeared widely across the country in personal appearances. Visit MonteHale.com

The J.B. Callaway and Sons Cotton Gin

The J.B. Callaway and Sons cotton gin, which opened in 1929, stands in Ringgold as a remembrance of days gone by. Former Catoosa County manager Jim Callaway said he started working with his dad J.B. Callaway and his brothers, J.W. and Richard, at age five. "People came to the gin in wagons, and some had trucks," Jim said. "They would line up down what is High Street now and up to Tennessee Street, almost all the way to Ringgold, and they would line up down Depot Street. My job was to walk from one block to another, and when people would come I put a number on them. That was my first job — making sure people did not get in front of other people when they went to the gin."

(Photo by Randall Franks)

ABOUT THE AUTHORS

Randall Franks

Randall Franks is an actor, an award winning singer musician, writer and photographer. He is

Franks

best known for his role as "Officer Randy Goode" on TV's *In the Heat of the Night*, now on WGNAmerica. He continues to appear in films and television and tours musically.

His latest CD release, "*An Appalachian Musical Revival*, is available at www.shareamericafoundation.org. He is a syndicated newspaper columnist and a city council member in Ringgold, Ga. (*Photo by Terry Pennington*)

Shirley Smith

Shirley Smith serves as executive director of Catoosa

Smith

County's Learning Center. In recognition of her leadership and her untiring efforts in making her dream of an adult learning center a reality for Catoosa County, the Board of Commissioners of Catoosa County

adopted a resolution officially naming the facility the Shirley Smith Learning Center.

Smith and her husband Wes, who is president of Northwest Georgia Bank, live just outside Ringgold. They have three adult children, Todd, Scott and

Krista Smith, and five grandchildren, Colton, Carter, Samuel, GraceAnn, and Wesley. Smith also serves the Catoosa County Foundation for the Arts. (*Photo by Darla Crawford*)

On the cover:
"Two Dozen Brown Eggs" © 2007 Cathy Cooksey, Ringgold, Ga. featuring Kitty and Pearl Bruce

Cathy Cooksey

Catoosa County artist Cathy Cooksey strives for realism in her paintings and in her life but she enjoys adding a bit of whimsy to her work.

She is a self-taught artist with no formal training, but she has always dabbled with her talent and considers it a gift.

Cooksey specializes in several areas using her original technique to create landscapes and portraits.

She painted murals at the Tunnel Hill Heritage Center and Fort Oglethorpe City Hall.

Cooksey is married to Thomas, and the mother of three children; Hunter, and two adult children; Heather and J.J. McCartney.

Front cover: (top, from left) Bill Cosby, Rebecca Holden, Sonny Shroyer, Donna Douglas, James Earl Jones, Lulu Roman, Alan Alda, Barbara Mandrell, (bottom) Stella Parton, Bill Anderson, Faith Hill, Randall Franks, Cristy Lane, Randy Travis, Dolly Parton and Charley Pride.
Back cover: (clockwise from bottom left) Vince Dooley, Barbara Dooley, Stonewall Jackson, Jeannie Seely, Roy Clark, Jett Williams, David Davis, Barbara Bush, Jesse McReynolds, Rosalynn Carter, Joe Diffie, Nancy Reagan, Rick Honeycutt, Lady Bird Johnson, Sheb Wooley, Laura Bush, Earle Wheeler of The Marksmen, Lorie Watkins of the Watkins Family, Alan Arbus, Dom DeLuise, Gigi Perreau, Larry Stephenson, and James Rogers All photos courtesy of the performers. Cover photo of Randall Franks by J. Alan Palmer

FOLKS YOU WOULD WRITE HOME ABOUT
MEETING

FOLKS YOU WOULD WRITE HOME ABOUT MEETING

Many celebrity participants shared more than one recipe. As you turn through the pages be sure to look for other favorites they shared.

Some other celebrities seen inside with their friends:

HOW TO FIND YOUR FAVORITES

HOW TO FIND YOUR FAVORITES

HOW TO FIND YOUR FAVORITES

Main Dish

HOW TO FIND YOUR FAVORITES